T0387570

Reddish Egret
at Bolivar Flats.

CHASING THE TIDE

ONE COUPLE'S 370-MILE TREK ACROSS THE BARRIER ISLANDS OF TEXAS

BY JAY KLEBERG WITH CHRISSY KLEBERG

Published by Greenleaf Book Group Press
Austin, Texas
www.gbgpress.com

Distributed by Greenleaf Book Group

For ordering information or special discounts for bulk purchases, please contact Greenleaf Book Group at PO Box 91869, Austin, TX 78709, 512.891.6100.

Design and composition by Greenleaf Book Group and Katy Baldock
Cover design by Travis Smith and Chad Tomlinson

Maps and Illustrations by Emma C. Schmidt

Photography by:
John Aldrich
Henry Davis
Skip Hobbie
Chrissy Kleberg
Jay Kleberg
Patrick Thrash

Publisher's Cataloging-in-Publication data is available.

Print ISBN: 979-8-88645-274-7

To offset the number of trees consumed in the printing of our books, Greenleaf donates a portion of the proceeds from each printing to the Arbor Day Foundation. Greenleaf Book Group has replaced over 50,000 trees since 2007.

Printed in Canada on acid-free paper

25 26 27 28 29 30 31 10 9 8 7 6 5 4 3 2 1

First Edition

TO SOPHIA, KATHERINE, AND AMELIA

BE KIND, CURIOUS, AND ADVENTUROUS

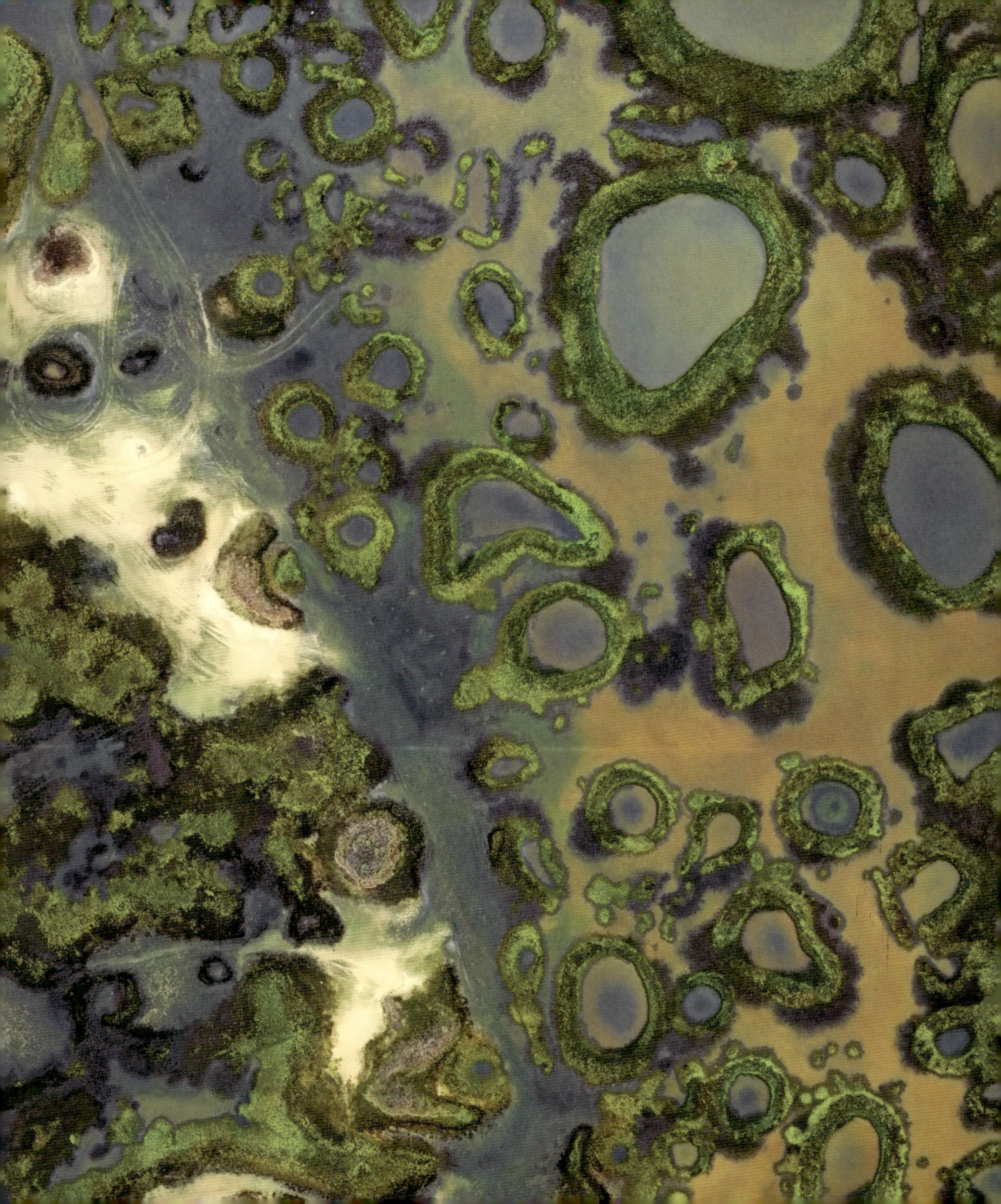

CONTENTS

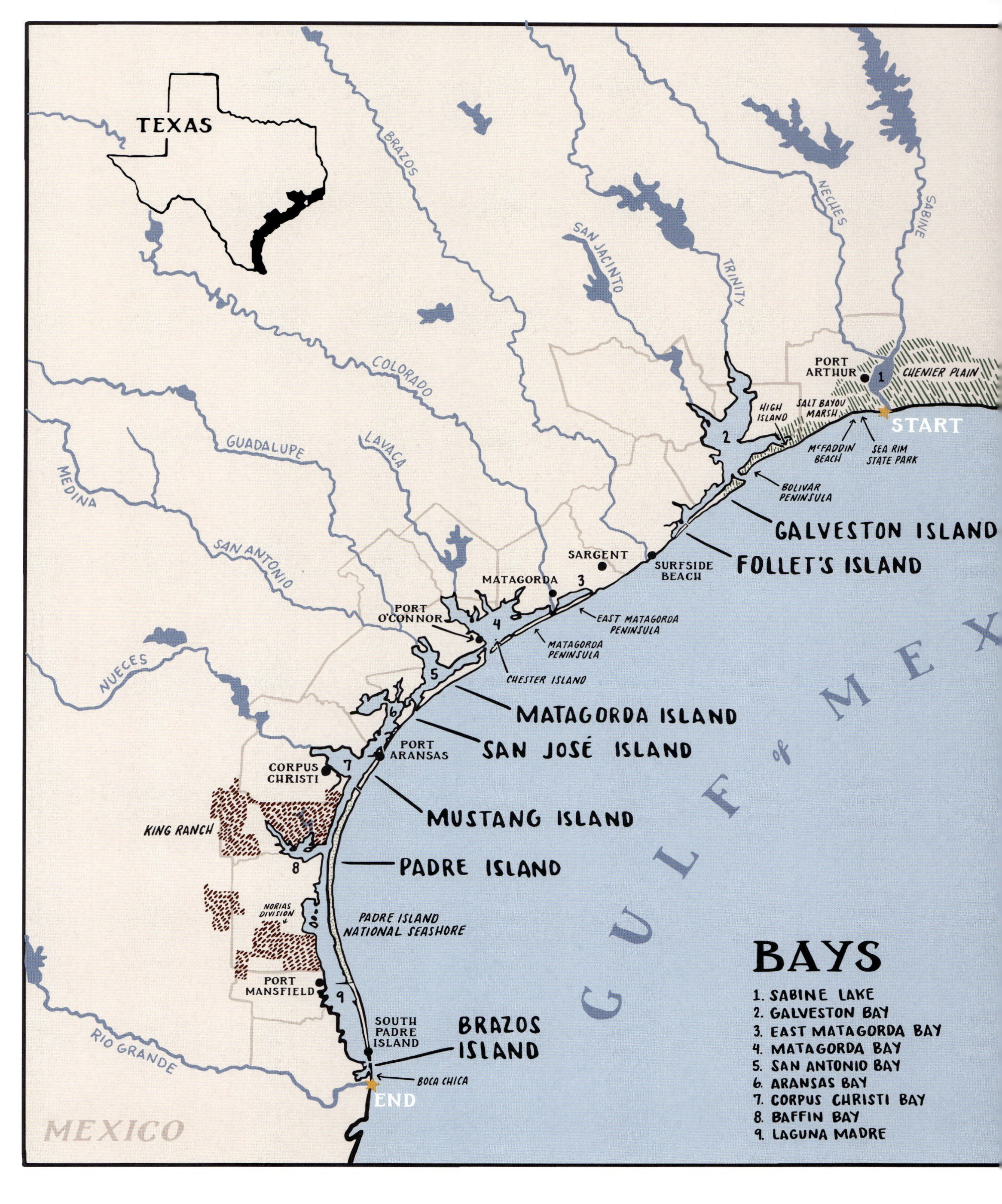
TEXAS
BRAZOS
NECHES
SABINE
SAN JACINTO
TRINITY
COLORADO
GUADALUPE
LAVACA
MEDINA
SAN ANTONIO
NUECES
RIO GRANDE
PORT ARTHUR
1
CHENIER PLAIN
HIGH ISLAND
SALT BAYOU MARSH
START
McFADDIN BEACH
SEA RIM STATE PARK
2
BOLIVAR PENINSULA
GALVESTON ISLAND
FOLLET'S ISLAND
SARGENT
SURFSIDE BEACH
MATAGORDA
3
EAST MATAGORDA PENINSULA
PORT O'CONNOR
4
MATAGORDA PENINSULA
CHESTER ISLAND
5
MATAGORDA ISLAND
6
SAN JOSÉ ISLAND
PORT ARANSAS
CORPUS CHRISTI
7
MUSTANG ISLAND
KING RANCH
8
PADRE ISLAND
NORIAS DIVISION
PADRE ISLAND NATIONAL SEASHORE
PORT MANSFIELD
9
SOUTH PADRE ISLAND
BRAZOS ISLAND
BOCA CHICA
END
MEXICO
GULF of MEX
BAYS
1. SABINE LAKE
2. GALVESTON BAY
3. EAST MATAGORDA BAY
4. MATAGORDA BAY
5. SAN ANTONIO BAY
6. ARANSAS BAY
7. CORPUS CHRISTI BAY
8. BAFFIN BAY
9. LAGUNA MADRE

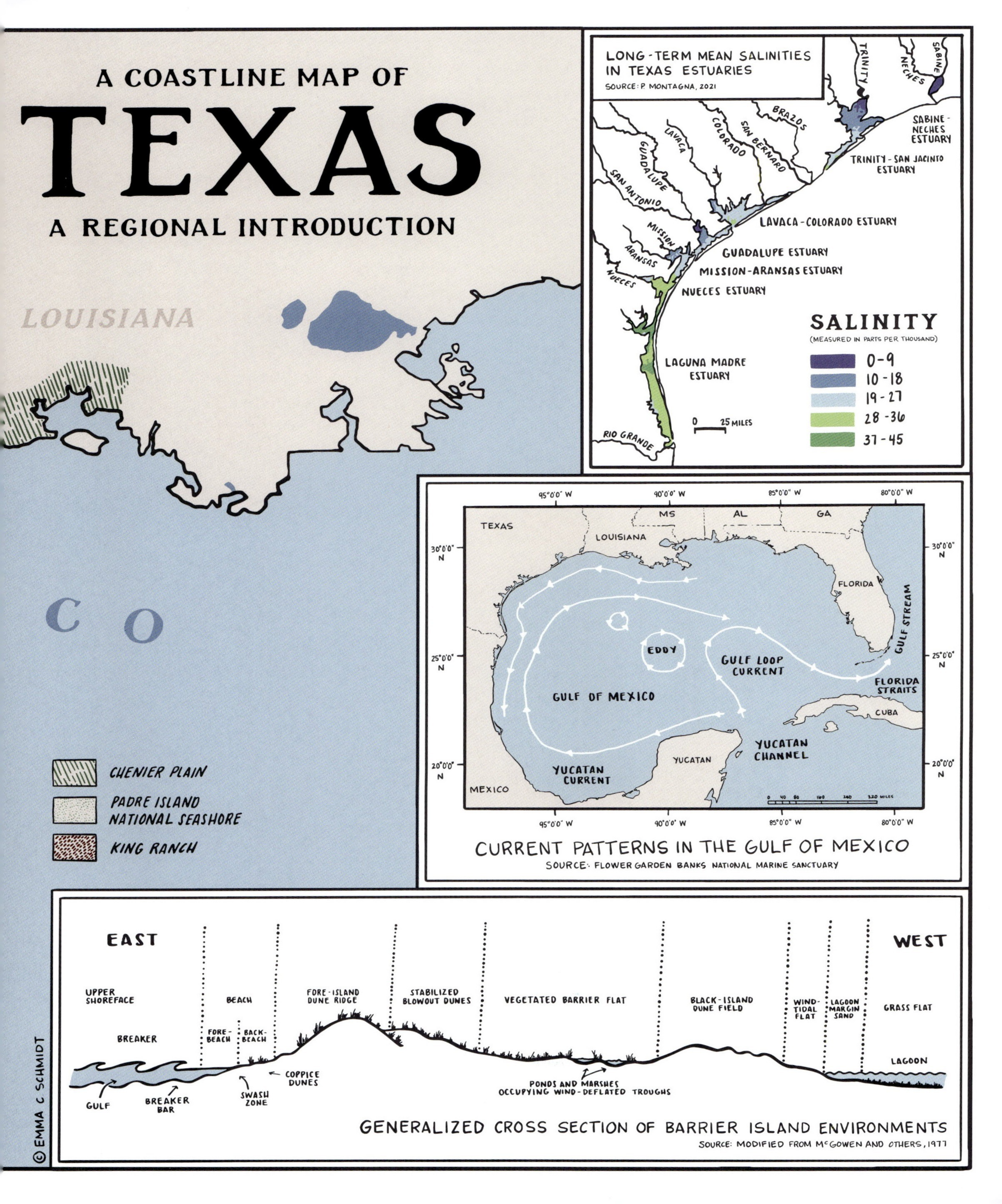
A COASTLINE MAP OF
TEXAS
A REGIONAL INTRODUCTION
LOUISIANA
C O
CHENIER PLAIN
PADRE ISLAND NATIONAL SEASHORE
KING RANCH
LONG-TERM MEAN SALINITIES IN TEXAS ESTUARIES
SOURCE: P. MONTAGNA, 2021
TRINITY
NECHES
SABINE
BRAZOS
COLORADO
SAN BERNARO
LAVACA
GUADALUPE
SAN ANTONIO
MISSION
ARANSAS
NUECES
SABINE-NECHES ESTUARY
TRINITY-SAN JACINTO ESTUARY
LAVACA-COLORADO ESTUARY
GUADALUPE ESTUARY
MISSION-ARANSAS ESTUARY
NUECES ESTUARY
LAGUNA MADRE ESTUARY
RIO GRANDE
0 25 MILES
SALINITY
(MEASURED IN PARTS PER THOUSAND)
0-9
10-18
19-27
28-36
37-45
95°0'0" W
90°0'0" W
85°0'0" W
80°0'0" W
30°0'0" N
25°0'0" N
20°0'0" N
TEXAS
LOUISIANA
MS
AL
GA
FLORIDA
GULF STREAM
EDDY
GULF LOOP CURRENT
FLORIDA STRAITS
CUBA
GULF OF MEXICO
YUCATAN CHANNEL
YUCATAN
YUCATAN CURRENT
MEXICO
0 40 80 160 240 320 MILES
CURRENT PATTERNS IN THE GULF OF MEXICO
SOURCE: FLOWER GARDEN BANKS NATIONAL MARINE SANCTUARY
EAST
WEST
UPPER SHOREFACE
BEACH
FORE-ISLAND DUNE RIDGE
STABILIZED BLOWOUT DUNES
VEGETATED BARRIER FLAT
BLACK-ISLAND DUNE FIELD
WIND-TIDAL FLAT
LAGOON MARGIN SAND
GRASS FLAT
BREAKER
FORE-BEACH
BACK-BEACH
LAGOON
COPPICE DUNES
PONDS AND MARSHES OCCUPYING WIND-DEFLATED TROUGHS
GULF
BREAKER BAR
SWASH ZONE
GENERALIZED CROSS SECTION OF BARRIER ISLAND ENVIRONMENTS
SOURCE: MODIFIED FROM McGOWEN AND OTHERS, 1977
© EMMA C. SCHMIDT

FOREWORD

Chrissy and Jay Kleberg have what my long-passed West Texas dad referred to as "grit," and that says something important about them because one thing those of us from West Texas know is sand and grit. We admire resolve and perseverance, which this book clearly embodies. Chrissy and Jay have both, so I am not surprised. They also have a lot more energy than most and a knack for telling the story of Texas' wild places uniquely, with compelling conviction and passion. *Chasing the Tide,* both the adventure and the book, could only have been done by them. Read this book and watch the documentary film series. You will see what I mean.

The Kleberg family is one of the most storied in Texas and is interlinked with its history and its coast through the King Ranch, running unencumbered along the Laguna Madre. The authors of this book sustain that family tradition. My own family came to Texas with Stephen Austin's "Old 300," but my part of the family headed away from the coast to West Texas in the mid-1840s. I love West Texas, but for me, it did not stick. I first saw the Texas coast when I was about six, fell in love with it when I hooked my first redfish, and never looked back. I have spent my 50-year career as a marine biologist on oceans all around the world, but I always came back to the Gulf of Mexico and especially the Texas coast. There is not much of it I have not been on or in, and I love it.

Generally, I regret books like this one being published because I would as soon keep to myself the hidden treasure that is the Texas coast. Yes, it is the hub of great industry and economic vitality from which we all benefit. That vitality also comes with all the downsides it can take to generate those advantages. Still, even today, I can be on the water all day and not see a soul but fish and birds, which does my own soul a lot of good. *Chasing the Tide* strikes a fair balance in its observations of our coast. Most importantly, it captures the feel of vast seagrass beds full of shrimp and trout, the coastal air full of birds, and the waving seas of salt marsh reaching over the horizon. That may be because I know it so well, but it comes to mind when reading Jay and Chrissy's account of their trek along the coast.

ABOVE
Wading birds feed at Bolivar Flats on Bolivar Peninsula.

Chasing the Tide is also a reminder to all of us that the Texas coast cannot be taken for granted. Texas and its long and diverse coast may be resilient, but it is not immutable. To our loss, the Texas coast of the original Kleberg and McKinney clans is not what we see today. Lacking that perspective, many Texans have come to think that the vigor and productivity of our coast can absorb any insult and come quickly back to "normal." Those of us who study our coast and its history know that is not true. We are on the edge of that cliff from which we may not come back once we step over. Chrissy and Jay have taken what they have learned from all the experts with whom they consulted, flavored it with the miles of beach they had trodden upon, and crafted a story that is readable and, more importantly, compelling. Hopefully, this book and all that it inspires will make us blink and take a step back from that cliff.

If you love the Texas coast, read this book and act. Show some grit! For Chrissy and Jay Kleberg and all of us that feel the same, we could ask for no more.

DR. LARRY D. MCKINNEY
SENIOR EXECUTIVE DIRECTOR (RETIRED)
HARTE RESEARCH INSTITUTE FOR GULF OF MEXICO STUDIES
TEXAS A&M UNIVERSITY–CORPUS CHRISTI

INTRODUCTION

Over the past decade, Chrissy and I have logged more than half a million miles driving through nearly every one of Texas' 254 counties. We spent many of those miles in separate vehicles, primarily because we had our own jobs and projects.

At the end of 2022, we found ourselves back home in Austin after a yearlong, nonstop trip around Texas, participating in the democratic process. Chrissy had been recruiting and managing volunteers for our friend's campaign for governor, and I had run for the statewide office of Texas Land Commissioner. While we lost both campaigns, we gained an appreciation for Texas' diversity of people and landscapes.

As the new year approached, we reminisced about our two decades together. We met in San Antonio in our mid 20s. I was getting my private pilot's license and soon returned to the Brazilian Amazon, where I lived and worked in land conservation and ecotourism. She had just graduated from Texas Tech with a range and wildlife management degree and set off for Hawaii to conduct field studies on avian malaria. The summer after we met, we flew a single-engine airplane 5,000 miles from the Amazon to Texas through the Caribbean, Bahamas, and the northern Gulf of Mexico.

Our relationship was rooted in adventure and a passion for land and wildlife conservation. While we have shared monthlong trips to the Oregon coast and Costa Rica with our three children, Chrissy and I longed for another adventure together. As we took stock of the past and contemplated the future, one thing became apparent—we were in love with long adventures. We also realized that we had spent a lot of time in nearly every one of Texas' 10 ecoregions, but there was a sliver of one region we'd hardly explored—the Texas Gulf Coast.

The Texas coast is unique in many ways—nearly every drop of water that falls in the state heads to its shoreline, millions of birds rely on its shallow waters and wetlands during their annual migrations, and seven barrier islands protect seven major bays that act as the nursing grounds for the Gulf of Mexico. Texas' 18 coastal counties account for a quarter of the state's population, lead the nation in oil and gas refining, account for half of all U.S. liquified natural gas exports, and are at the forefront of new energy technologies like hydrogen production and carbon capture and storage.

Texas' coastal region embodies what the state is and aspires to be—breathtaking and gritty, storied and inspiring, expansive and eclectic—and the region is under imminent threat. The people and wildlife on the Texas Gulf Coast reside on the front lines of a rapidly changing climate. Due to currents influenced by wind, ocean warming, and melting Antarctic ice, the sea level is rising faster on the shores of Texas than almost anywhere else in the world. Texas' shoreline also experiences some of the highest coastal erosion rates in the nation due to sea level rise, subsidence (the land is sinking), and storm surges. The beaches and coastline are retreating at an average rate of 4 feet per year. In the past century, Texans also drained, paved, and built over half of their coastal wetlands that serve as natural storm and flood buffers.

Along with an eroding coastline and the loss of wetlands, Texans converted over 99 percent of native coastal prairie to cropland, residential and commercial developments, and infrastructure. These changes to the landscape place coastal communities and ecosystems at risk due to rising seas and more extreme storms. Texans are already feeling the impacts. The state leads the nation in billion-dollar disasters. From 1980 to 2024, Texas experienced 171 billion-dollar weather and climate disaster events. Among all severe weather events in the state, the most expensive were 14 storms that hit the coast, costing the state over $234 billion in damages.

Chrissy and I wanted to learn more about the barrier islands and communities fronting the Gulf of Mexico. In doing so, we thought it would elevate the region's importance, what is at stake, and what can be done to balance economic progress with healthy ecosystems. We decided that walking would be the best way to immerse ourselves and to cover 370 miles of beaches, islands, and peninsulas and cross 15 passes, river mouths, and ship channels. To add significance to the endeavor, we discovered that no one had walked the length of the state's islands and peninsulas in a single attempt.

A few weeks after committing to the task, I had a chance meeting with the leadership at Austin PBS. We were brainstorming ways to encourage and invest in content creators. Toward the end of the meeting, Luis Patiño, Austin PBS CEO, asked me if I had come across any new film projects. I was part of the team that produced the feature-length documentaries *The River and the Wall* and *Deep in the Heart: A Texas Wildlife Story* with Ben Masters, Katy

Baldock, and the Fin & Fur Films team. I mentioned that Chrissy and I planned to walk the coast but were debating whether or not to film it because of the challenges of doing so in a remote and sometimes harsh environment. Additionally, we weren't sure we wanted to take on a film project without having a distribution partner who could reach a broad audience. Luis asked me to come back to him and his staff with a pitch for a documentary film (after completing the walk, we decided to pivot from a 60-minute film to a 6-part, 180-minute docuseries because we realized we had so many stories to tell).

In early 2023, Chrissy and I met with John Aldrich and Skip Hobbie, who immediately agreed to join the team. We first met John while working together on *The River and the Wall* and then worked with Skip on *Deep in the Heart*. John is originally from Florida, went to film school at the University of Texas at Austin, then obtained his master's in documentary filmmaking from the University of Florida. He has worked on several feature-length documentaries and began his career as a National Geographic producer, editor, and cameraman. He came on the team to edit, film, co-write, and co-produce *Chasing the Tide*.

Skip is a wildlife cinematographer with a degree from the University of Texas at Austin and has filmed all over the world for *National Geographic*, the BBC, PBS, Netflix, and on independent features. Skip agreed to serve as *Chasing the Tide*'s co-producer and director of photography. We put a budget together and returned to Austin PBS to ask if they would distribute the film. They said yes, and we immediately got to work.

Our first task was determining how long it would take us to walk the coastline and where we would start and finish. We spent the first two months poring over maps, counting and checking the total mileage, and talking to contacts at Texas Parks and Wildlife Department, U.S. Fish and Wildlife Service, National Park Service, private landowners, fishing guides, researchers, and local beachcombers. Besides the physical task of walking 370 miles, we also had to consider our other obligations—to our daughters, who'd have a combination of family, friends, and babysitters to help keep them alive and in school, and to those who recently hired me to lead a nonprofit coastal conservation organization. We decided to start at the Texas/Louisiana border, walk about 20 miles a day, allow for three rest days (which turned into only one), and complete the journey in the first three weeks of October 2023.

Next, we put together a production schedule. Between mid-January 2023 and the end of September 2023, we executed more than a dozen wildlife shoots and another dozen interviews with scientists, local leaders, and coastal residents at locations from the Texas border with Louisiana to the border with Mexico.

On the Upper Coast, near Port Arthur and Houston, we heard from community leaders about the completion of the largest coastal restoration project in the country and efforts to fortify the coast by launching the largest public works project in U.S. history. On Galveston Island, we met residents and scientists rallying to save the lost descendants of the endangered red wolf. Farther down the coast, we met members of an Indigenous group, thought to be extinct, who are now reconnecting after a century in the shadows. Near the town of Port Aransas on Mustang Island, we interviewed wildlife researchers and anglers who have joined forces to protect the nation's last remaining wild oyster reefs. On South Padre Island, near the Texas-Mexico border, we spent time with members of a conservation organization who are part of a binational effort to restore the population of the most endangered sea turtle in the world.

This book is a record of our nine months of preparation and three weeks hiking the Texas Gulf Coast. We also include journal entries adapted from audio recordings captured during our 21-day trek. By walking Texas' shoreline, we hoped to better understand its character. What we learned is that every mile of the Texas coast is different. It's ever-changing, and it's beautiful. Those who live here, with the sea at their doorstep, have figured that out. It's the responsibility of those who don't live on the coast to appreciate its significance, care for it, and support efforts to keep it wild and accessible for all Texans for all time.

We intend for this book and film series to encourage more people to think about Texas as a coastal state and that wherever they live in the Lone Star State, their actions and choices impact the Gulf. Texas' coast is at the frontier of our energy and economic future, adaptation to changes in our climate, and the delicate balance between population growth and a healthy environment. One thing that we learned in writing this book and making this documentary film series is that Texans are resilient. We hope that our wild things and wild places share the same trait.

A NOTE FROM CHRISSY

Growing up in San Antonio, I never really thought of Texas as being a coastal state. Aside from a few trips to Port Aransas and Galveston with my family and a spring break trip to South Padre Island in college, I had never explored much of the Texas coast.

During and shortly after college, I landed field jobs searching for snails in a Puerto Rican rainforest, hiking many miles over volcanic rock trapping mosquitoes in Hawaii, driving airboats and wading through alligator-infested swamps in the Florida Everglades, and living in a one-room camphouse with no electricity or running water in the west Texas desert monitoring Aplomado Falcons.

Now in my forties and married with three kids, I had only added Port O'Connor and Padre Island National Seashore to my list of short trips to the Texas Gulf Coast.

I have always said yes to everything. So, in early December 2022, when Jay proposed that we walk Texas' barrier islands together, I immediately agreed. It didn't hurt that we were sitting in a bar in Mexico City, reminiscing about the last couple of decades of marriage and contemplating the future. I said yes, partly because I subconsciously longed for the adventurous life I had led before we married.

Our relationship began as an adventure. After a brief courtship, I joined Jay in Brazil, where he'd been working in conservation and ecotourism. We crisscrossed the Amazon for a month and flew a single-engine airplane 5,000 miles back to Texas, island-hopping along the way with Jay in the pilot's seat. Although rich with children, friends, and work, life seemed to fly by in the intervening years. I didn't know until that night in Mexico City that I had been waiting for the chance to explore the unknown again.

While we hadn't planned to document the trip, a chance meeting with the leadership team at PBS Austin in late December sparked our interest in shining a light on the Texas coast through film and photography.

We realized early on that to capture wildlife footage and interview experts, we needed more than just the 21 days we planned to walk the coast that October. I seized the opportunity to live out my lifelong dream of being a wildlife photographer and filmmaker. By January 2023, we had assembled a team, and I was in the field scouting and learning to shoot from some of the best wildlife cinematographers in the business.

ABOVE
(Left) Trapping mosquitoes for avian malaria testing for the U.S. Geological Survey, Hawaii Volcanoes National Park.
(Right) Monitoring the Snail Kite population in the Florida Everglades for the University of Florida.

While capturing the coast on film was a priority for me, preparing to walk 370 miles in three weeks was little more than an afterthought. I guess jumping to say "yes" at critical junctures in my life also comes with a hefty dose of optimism and expectation that it will all work out. The beginning, however, always comes so soon.

I was so focused on our monthly trips to different parts of the coast to film that I left the physical preparation until the latter part of the summer. When it came time to get in shape, the only time I could find between the hectic shoot schedule and responsibilities at home came when our three girls were finally out of school. By that time, summer temperatures were in the low 100s, so Jay and I set out at night on hikes through the trails and streets of Austin.

The night before we started our trek down the coast, I couldn't sleep. Would the girls be alright without us? Would our two dogs and three cats get fed? Can we actually pull this off? Did I bring the right shoes? Will I be able to walk 20 miles, let alone 370? Will our marriage survive this? Suffice it to say I was awake when my alarm went off at 4 a.m.

The first day was difficult. It was really hot, and the terrain was more wetland than beach. We completed 12.5 miles of our 20-mile goal. While falling short of our desired mileage was demoralizing, knowing that we might let our team down was hard to stomach.

After a tough start, we welcomed the cooling effect that arrived with several days of thunderstorms. The rain kept the team from filming but allowed us to focus on the journey. By the time we reached the West End of Galveston Island, our bodies had become accustomed to walking up to 12 hours a day. By the fifth day, we were free of aches and worries and could finally focus on the wonderful changes in our surroundings. The girls and pets were never far from my thoughts or my phone. Once the school day ended, I spent much of the days'

ABOVE
Some of the many treasures found on our 21-day trek.

remaining hours ordering groceries, sharing stories over FaceTime, and checking to make sure their homework was complete.

While Jay may have walked 370 miles, I'm pretty confident that I walked close to 390 miles. I fell in love with beachcombing and zig-zagged across every mile of beach. Every day differed from the next, and I couldn't wait to see what the tides would leave behind. From sea glass to shark's teeth, acorn barnacles, sand dollars, sea beans, or all kinds of shells – Lightning whelks the size of my hand, sundials, scallops, angel wings, lettered olives, pen shells, and so many more.

We met so many people who came to our aid with a place to stay for the night or a boat ride across a river mouth. We all became fast friends. Some volunteer their time rescuing people and their vehicles from the sand or mud, some clean up trash from the beaches, and so many others have been fishing and recreating on the coast with their family and friends for generations. I was blown away by how many people have a deep love of the Texas coast, appreciate all it has to offer, and have dedicated their lives to conserving coastal habitats and wildlife.

Adventures like this remind me of the simple things. They remind me to live intentionally and to notice who's walking next to me on life's journey. It doesn't take a 370-mile walk to figure this out, but it's a great excuse for a change of pace.

While the Texas coast may have one of the longest coastlines in the country, it's the people and the smallest of things that make it so special. I have a greater appreciation for the coastal state I'm lucky to call home.

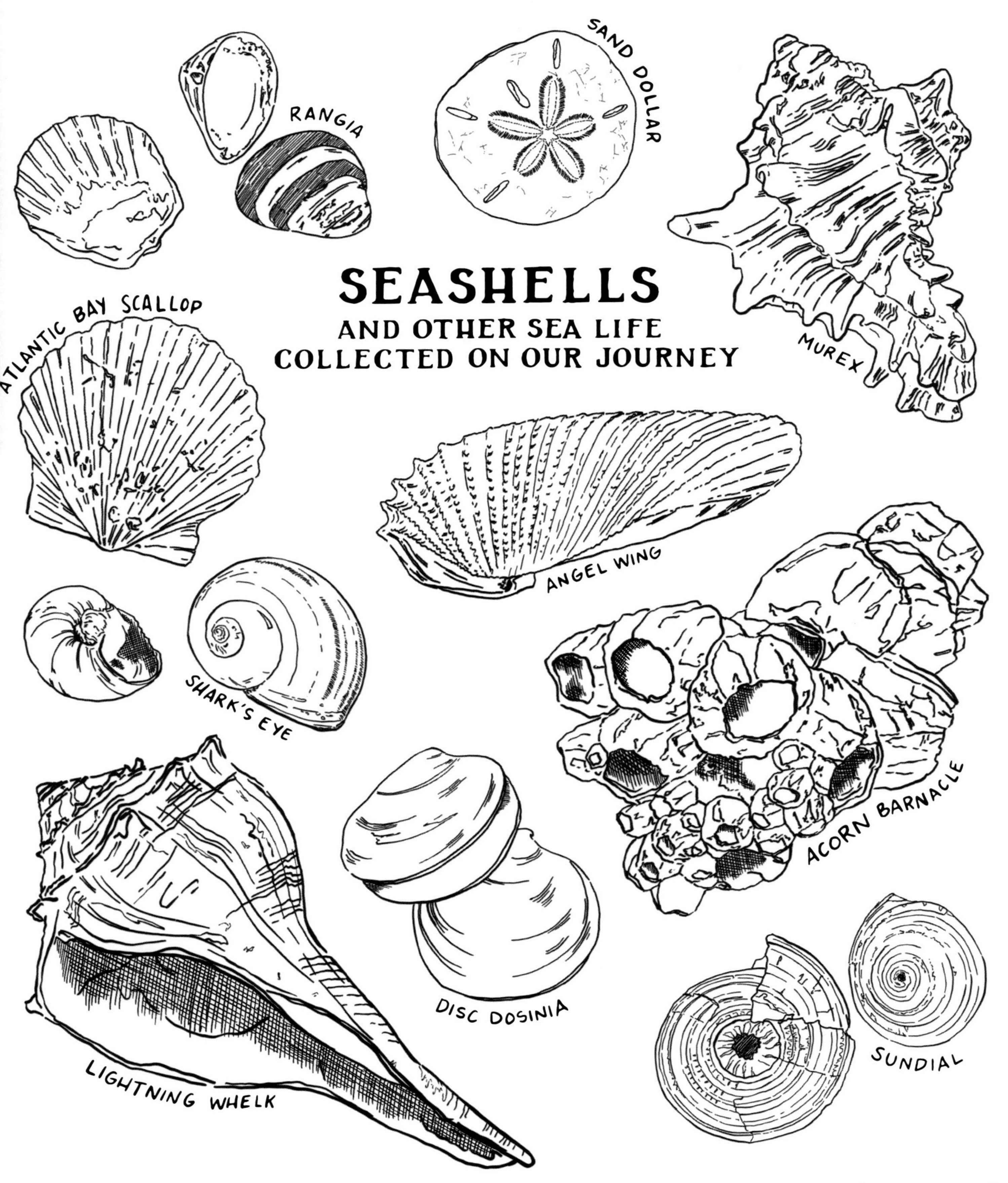
SEASHELLS
AND OTHER SEA LIFE
COLLECTED ON OUR JOURNEY
RANGIA
SAND DOLLAR
MUREX
ATLANTIC BAY SCALLOP
ANGEL WING
SHARK'S EYE
ACORN BARNACLE
DISC DOSINIA
LIGHTNING WHELK
SUNDIAL

CHAPTER 1

THE CHENIER PLAIN

RESTORATION ON THE UPPER COAST

Day: 1
Miles walked: 12.5
Miles remaining: 357.5

October 1, 2023

We woke up at 4:30 a.m. today and finished walking at 4:30 p.m. The first 12.5 miles were tough, and we got pretty emotional leaving the girls. It was hard knowing that we wouldn't see them for at least two weeks and be apart from them for the better part of three weeks.

The plan was to walk 20 miles today, which is set to be our goal for the entire three-week hike. But on about four and a half hours of sleep, after nine months of planning, pressing hard to get this project funded and production underway, scouting the most challenging passes and least walkable areas, making connections with experts, and ensuring that all of our other responsibilities with our children

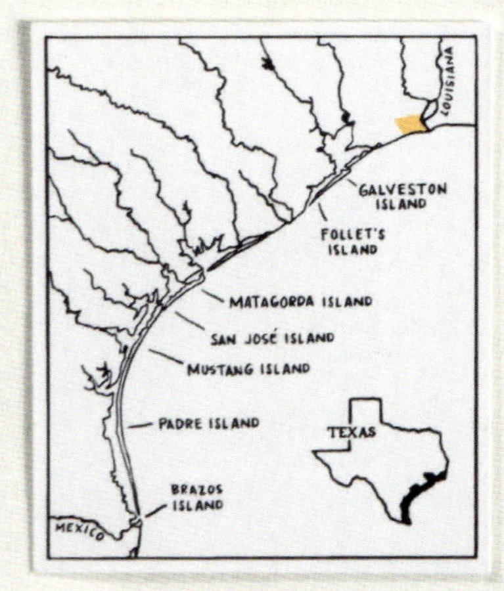

and work were taken care of and sewn up so that we could embark on this journey... well, it just added up and we were tired today.

The terrain made walking difficult. It's a mixture of crushed shell and an elevated shelf above sea level. It can get deep at times and be a struggle to get through. Some parts of the shoreline consist of a layer of marshy peat, a mulch-type material, which has washed out to sea and settled on the water's edge.

We passed shorebirds feeding on worms and clams in the soft, black muck. At times, we encountered areas with a clay layer that had settled into a hard, dark, black, lava-looking mud beneath the sand and was exposed by the tide.

In some parts, this mud shelf has completely eroded away, and the shell ridge is gone, so there's just marsh grass that stands about chest-deep on islands of marsh muck. In those marshy areas, the mosquitoes were thick, big and voracious. We could only walk 12.5 miles today, but we had to stop.

Salt marsh sediment settles on the beach at Sea Rim State Park.

When Chrissy and I first looked at satellite images of the Texas coast in December of 2022, the eastern shore of Texas' barrier islands appeared to be a continuous line of raw, sugar-colored sand protecting mostly grass-covered dunes and marsh. The occasional narrow pass linking the open waters of the Gulf of Mexico to shallow bays broke up long stretches of coastline. Our 370-mile journey along the barrier islands appeared to simply be a very, very long walk on the beach.

As we committed to the project and began planning in earnest, we settled on a north-to-south trajectory thanks to a suggestion by John Aldrich. He suggested that starting on the Upper Coast, at the Texas/Louisiana border, would provide opportunities to begin the film by highlighting society's imprint on this part of the state. In the first few days of hiking, we'd be passing through a region with more than five million people and the largest petrochemical complex in the world. The end of the journey and the film would be both a look back in time at a more pristine coast on Padre Island National Seashore and a glimpse into the future at Boca Chica, where SpaceX intends to carry people and cargo to the Moon and Mars.

After looking more closely at the maps and making a few calls to locals in the Port Arthur area, we stumbled upon our first logistical challenge. The shoreline near Sabine Pass on the Louisiana/Texas border had eroded so much over the years that there were places in the first 30 miles of the trip where the beach had disappeared. The entire project suddenly fell apart on one assumption—that we'd at least have a shoreline to walk.

We also found that while the region was highly populated, there were still large, intact ecosystems, and they were under attack from the effects of a changing climate and a landscape altered by human engineering. In addition to erosion, saltwater intrusion, sea-level rise, and the construction of navigation canals had contributed to the loss of this coastal marsh, like others in Texas, for nearly a century. The more we researched, the more we began to understand these threats and piece together the story of a 20-year effort, the Salt Bayou Watershed Restoration Project, to protect this salt marsh and the Chenier Plain, one of the most significant ecosystems in the Western Hemisphere. When we set off on our walk, we would be traversing one of Texas' newest beaches, McFaddin Beach, and the last stage of the Salt Bayou project—one of the largest coastal restoration projects in the nation. At the other end of the Texas Gulf Coast near South Padre Island, we would pass the Bahia Grande Restoration

RIGHT
Walking the eastern edge of the Salt Bayou ecosystem at the Texas/Louisiana border.

Project, also one of the largest wetland restoration projects in the U.S. Two of the country's leading conservation efforts at opposite ends of Texas' shoreline.

Chenier plains occur in different parts of the world—the northern coast of South America, the river deltas of East China, and the mud coasts of Vietnam and West Africa. A chenier plain is a series of sandy or shelly ridges called "cheniers," many more than 10 feet high, separated by clayey or silty marsh deposits. The word chenier is derived from the Cajun French word *chène*, meaning oak, the dominant tree growing on the crests of cheniers in southwestern Louisiana and Texas.

The Gulf Coast's Chenier Plain is an ecological system that stretches along the northwestern Gulf of Mexico, covering nearly 200 miles from Galveston, Texas, to Vermilion Bay, Louisiana. The area encompasses over 6.5 million acres and consists of former coastal tallgrass prairies and marshlands.

This mosaic of oak forests and shallow wetlands fulfills several critical roles, including safeguarding coastal communities against storm surges, acting as a nursery for vital fisheries, and providing essential habitat for migratory waterfowl, shorebirds, and wading birds. Its coastal ridges and adjacent marshes play a pivotal role in mitigating floods and protecting inland areas by slowing the force of the waves and limiting the depth of the rising waters. Trees found on ridges serve as crucial rest stops for millions of songbirds during migratory journeys across the Gulf of Mexico. Over 360 bird species rely on this coastal ecosystem for breeding, migrating, and making it through the winter.

The Chenier Plain started to form about 3,000 years ago when the mouth of the Mississippi River shifted to the west, bringing an increase in sediment to southwestern Louisiana and deep southeast Texas. These sediments built marshes out into the Gulf. During periods of low sediment input from the Mississippi, wave action reworked the Gulf-facing sediments into ridges until the next pulse of sediment built marsh farther out into the Gulf again, resulting in the characteristic series of ridges.

The mouth of the Mississippi has shifted repeatedly since this series of ridges began to form, causing periods in which the beach built up slowly and periods of rapid marsh expansion

LEFT

(Top) The Chenier Plain ecosystem with the Gulf of Mexico in the background just south of Port Arthur. (Bottom) The Eastern edge of the Salt Bayou Watershed with Sabine Pass and Louisiana in the background.

into the Gulf. In this way, the once broad bay of the Sabine and Neches Rivers was cut off from the Gulf by wetlands.

The Salt Bayou Marsh ecosystem lies within the larger Chenier Plain region of the northern Gulf of Mexico. It is the largest contiguous estuarine marsh complex in Texas and is among the most productive ecosystems on earth. The system covers approximately 139,000 acres in Jefferson County. It is primarily protected as public land by McFaddin and Texas Point National Wildlife Refuges, J.D. Murphree Wildlife Management Area, and Sea Rim State Park. For thousands of years, this wetland ecosystem was protected from salty Gulf waters by beaches and dunes and fueled by the natural flow of fresh water between connected shallow lakes and small bayous.

This delicate exchange of fresh and salt water, sediment, and organisms began changing with alterations to the land in the mid-1800s. Historically, the Salt Bayou watershed was predominantly a fresh water-to-intermediate system, meaning the marsh was subject to periodic pulses of salt water. However, by 1900, the development of a rail line and the dredging of a shallow-draft boat canal resulted in salt water migrating into nearby freshwater rice farms and blocking the natural flow of water across the marsh into Sabine Lake and the Gulf of Mexico.

By the 1930s, the Gulf Intracoastal Waterway (GIWW) and the Sabine-Neches Waterway had been completed. With the construction of the GIWW, the overland freshwater flows that used to drain from the northern to the southern part of the watershed were cut off, leading to the elimination of almost half of Salt Bayou's watershed and a decline in overall biodiversity. Moreover, the GIWW acted as a significant conduit for salt water to reach areas that rarely experienced tidal influx before. As a result, prolonged exposure to salt water caused the death of many salt-intolerant plants. In certain regions, more salt-tolerant plants replaced those that perished, while vegetated marshes transformed into open water in several locations. Around the same period, oil and gas production commenced near the Clam Lake area, close to present-day Sea Rim State Park, southwest of Port Arthur. The large-scale extraction of groundwater and oil triggered the activation of a fault line, leading to land subsidence, or sinking, and the conversion of marshland into open water.

RIGHT
Much of the Texas coast is undeveloped, and two of the nation's largest coastal restoration projects in the country are found at opposite ends of the state's Gulf of Mexico shoreline.

CONSERVING THE COAST

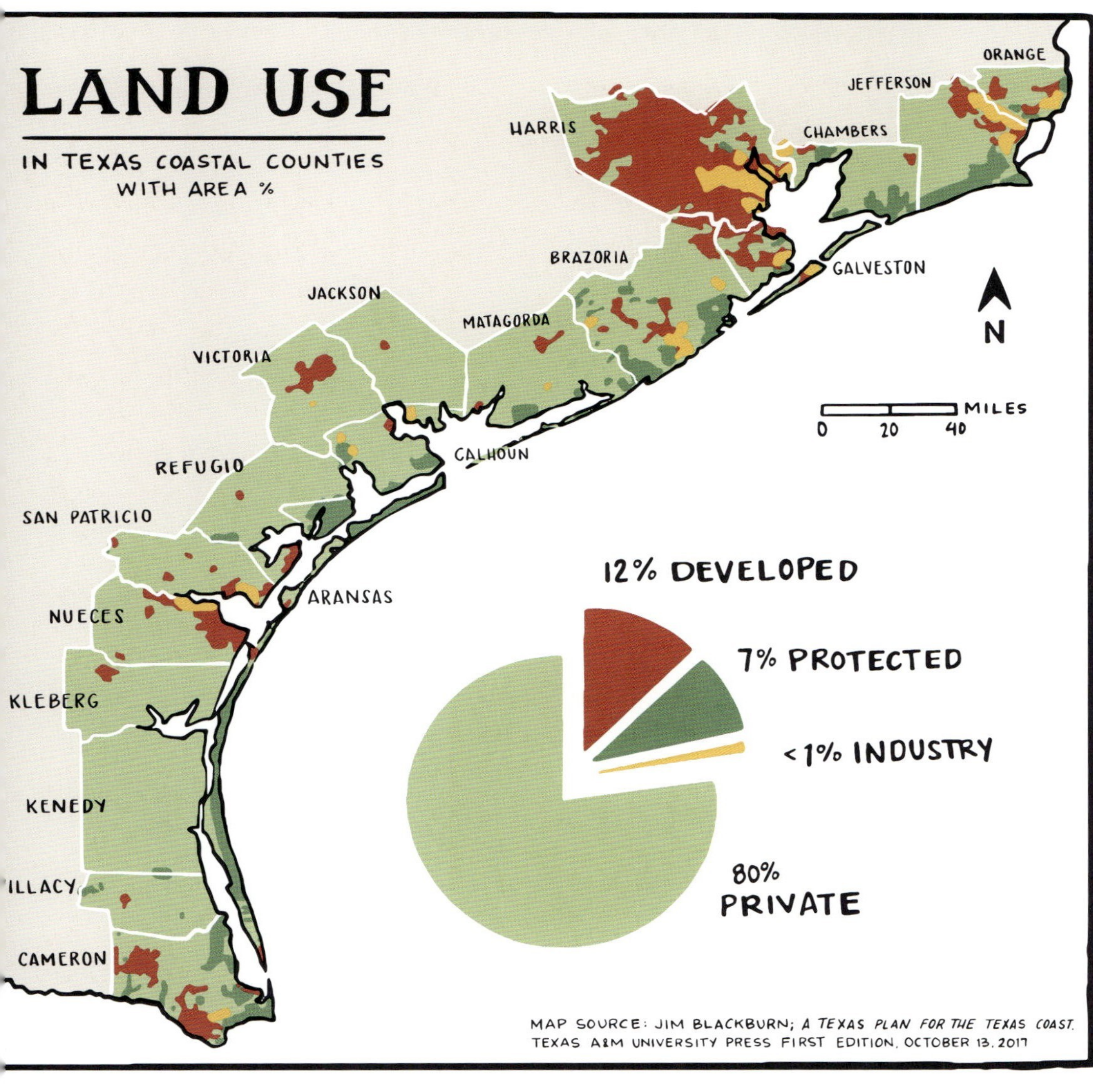

MAP SOURCE: JIM BLACKBURN; *A TEXAS PLAN FOR THE TEXAS COAST.* TEXAS A&M UNIVERSITY PRESS FIRST EDITION. OCTOBER 13, 2017

MORE THAN 700,000 ACRES OF TEXAS COASTAL LAND IS PERMANENTLY CONSERVED BY PUBLIC AND PRIVATE GROUPS.

FIG 1.

THE BAHIA GRANDE RESTORATION PROJECT HAS BEEN A DECADES-LONG COOPERATIVE TO RESTORE 10,000 ACRES OF CRITICAL WETLAND AND SHALLOW WATER HABITAT FOR WILDLIFE AND FISHERIES.

THE PROJECT ADDS TO A 105,000-ACRE CORRIDOR OF FEDERAL AND STATE CONSERVATION LANDS AND MORE THAN 2 MILLION ACRES OF PRIVATE RANCHLAND.

FIG 2.

THE SALT BAYOU ECOSYSTEM IS THE LARGEST CONTIGUOUS ESTUARINE MARSH COMPLEX IN TEXAS.

BEGINNING IN THE EARLY 2000s, LOCAL, STATE, FEDERAL, AND CONSERVATION LEADERS BEGAN RESTORING THE NATURAL HYDROLOGY OF SALT BAYOU AND A 20-MILE DUNE AND BEACH COMPLEX THAT BECAME ONE OF THE NATION'S LARGEST COASTAL RESTORATION PROJECTS.

MAP SOURCE: SALT BAYOU MARSH WORKSHOP; SALT BAYOU WATERSHED RESTORATION DRAFT CONCEPTUAL PLAN, MAY 6, 2013.

G 1. THE BAHIA GRANDE

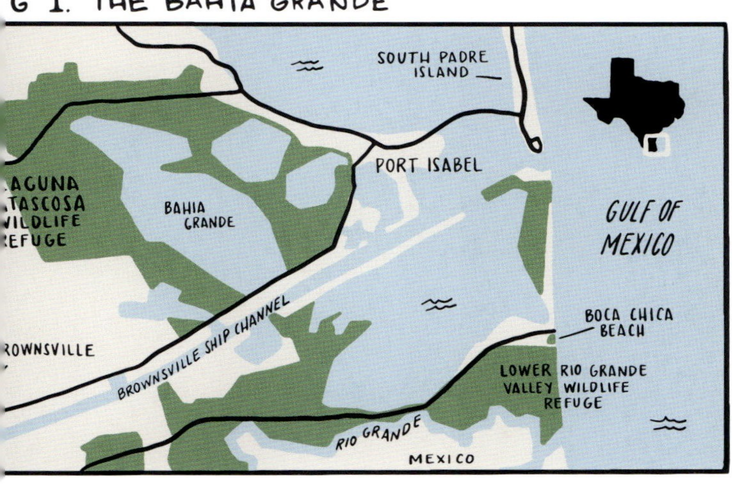

FIG 2. THE SALT BAYOU

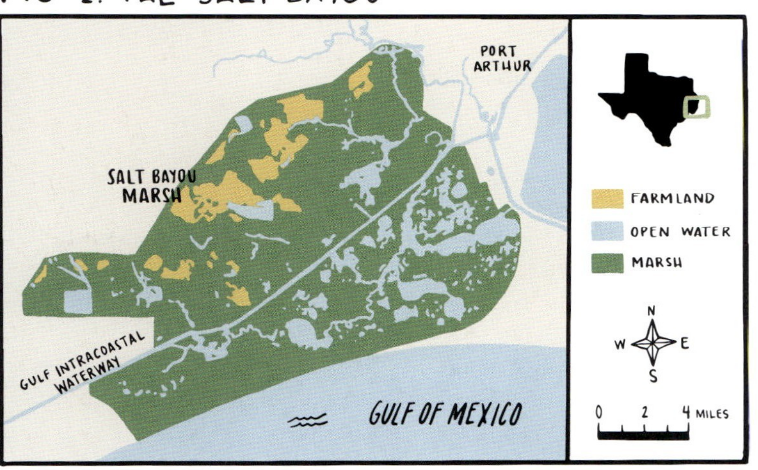

Pioneering salt grass establishes new marsh habitat at Texas Point National Wildlife Refuge.

ABOVE
Dredge pipe connects centuries-old sand deposits 1.5 miles offshore to the restoration of beach and dunes at McFaddin National Wildlife Refuge.

Engineering advances are not the only threat to the Salt Bayou Marsh. The rising sea and more intense storms have also weakened and degraded it. The National Oceanic and Atmospheric Agency tracks the relative sea level trends at Sabine Pass at 6 millimeters per year from 1958 to 2020. In comparison, the global sea level rise in the 20th century was 1.7 millimeters per year. This part of the Upper Coast has also suffered from substantial shoreline erosion and retreat, significantly degrading the historic barrier/beach dune system. On average, the shoreline in Jefferson County has been retreating nine feet per year, with land loss rates averaging nearly 36 acres per year.[1]

All of these blows to the marsh ecosystem lowered its resiliency, making it more vulnerable to extreme weather events. Hurricane Rita hit the Chenier Plain in 2005 and reduced the elevated beach ridge to a point where it can no longer protect marshes from high tide and storm surges. Hurricane Ike, which made landfall over Galveston on September 13, 2008, resulted in the complete loss of 3,700 acres of land in Jefferson County and destroyed the coastal road connecting High Island with Sabine Pass. After years of abuse, the marsh's future was uncertain. Unfortunately, it took a manmade disaster in the Gulf and a group of public and private partners to chart and complete a more optimistic path that included the funding and restoration of a broken ecosystem.

In the aftermath of Hurricane Ike, combined forces from Jefferson County, Texas Parks and Wildlife Department, Texas General Land Office, United States Fish and Wildlife Service, Ducks Unlimited, Texas Audubon, National Fish and Wildlife Foundation, Texas Parks and Wildlife Foundation, private companies, and others began working to restore the Salt Bayou Marsh. State and federal partners funded the $156 million project with settlement funds from the 2010 Deepwater Horizon oil spill.

ABOVE
We walked an eroded shoreline at the edge of the Salt Bayou Marsh as a ship traveled through Sabine Pass to Port Arthur.

The road map for their work, the Salt Bayou Watershed Restoration Plan, included the installation of two siphon pumps to restore Salt Bayou's natural hydrology and a 20-mile dune and beach complex to reduce storm surge and flooding impacts. The siphons allow excess fresh water from the marsh north of the GIWW to flow into the marsh south of the GIWW, which has been cut off from this source of freshwater inflow for more than 75 years.

While implementing the restoration plan, Hurricane Harvey hit, taking people's lives and threatening the region's economy. The hurricane also brought national attention since the Port Arthur–Beaumont area produces 12 percent of the nation's gasoline, 20 percent of its diesel fuel, 50 percent of its commercial aviation fuel, and 70 percent of its military aviation fuel. Harvey emphasized the need for continued investment in ecosystem restoration to protect against the next flood or hurricane.

ABOVE
Sea Rim State Park sits at the eastern edge of the newly restored McFaddin Beach.

RIGHT
Shorebirds and colonial waterbirds took advantage of the 20 miles of new and undisturbed beach at McFaddin.

In early October 2023, Chrissy and I were some of the first to make footprints on the final piece of the Salt Bayou Watershed Restoration Project—a restored McFaddin Beach. The ongoing construction project stretched nearly 20 miles. To our right we saw a new line of dunes, and underfoot was a massive beach that extended as much as 300 feet out into the Gulf of Mexico. Crews dredged sand from an old, submerged riverbed a mile and a half offshore. The irony is not lost on us. Ancient alluvial sand deposits buried by rising seas 7,000 to 9,000 years ago are modern Texans' first line of defense against sea level rise and climate change.

The construction of new dunes and beaches could give the marsh a chance to flourish again. The last 15 years of work to restore this ecosystem could help the people, communities, and wildlife of this region stand their ground. It might also simply postpone a managed retreat from the coastline. As we learned through this nearly monthlong journey, most Texans living on the coast prefer to fight.

CHAPTER 2

HIGH ISLAND

A GULF COAST REFUGE

Day: 4
Miles walked: 84
Miles remaining: 286

October 4, 2023

We're on the West End of Galveston Island tonight, having hiked just under 20 miles today, starting on the east end of the seawall. It's been raining with lightning and wind gusts up to 30 miles an hour for the past couple of days. While it prevents the film crew — John Aldrich, Skip Hobbie, and Patrick Thrash from filming —

the wind and rain are a welcome reprieve from the challenge of walking in 93-degree heat and 90% humidity.

Galveston built its seawall after the 1900 hurricane completely

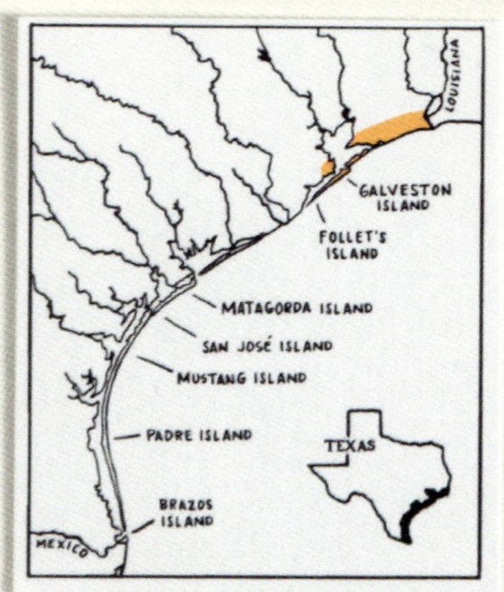

wiped out the island. In contrast to the quiet beach backed by homes on Bolivar Peninsula, the Galveston Island shoreline is an expression of determination, engineering, and capitalism. The seawall stretches 10 miles and stands 17 feet

We made it to Sea Isle Beach on the West End of Galveston Island at sundown. While our bodies hold up through six hours of walking each day, they begin to break down shortly thereafter. Our feet, knees, and backs hurt from carrying backpacks filled with 10 pounds of water, a few pounds of shells, and assorted snacks — beef jerky, tuna fish packs, Sour Patch Kids, and salt and vinegar pistachios.

Hopefully, our bodies get used to these 10 and 12 hours of walking every day. Minor ailments turn into big problems on these long journeys. We have a day off scheduled in Surfside Beach in a couple of days, but we're thinking of heading back up the coast to make up the mileage we skipped at McFaddin Beach. All in all, we still have about 300 miles left and the more remote stretches without crew support lie ahead.

above the beach with a sidewalk and a four-lane boulevard running its length.

A few miles from the east end of the seawall, we passed the remnants of the 300-foot pier that was the site of the Balinese Room, a high-end nightclub and gambling destination in the 1930s and 1940s that hosted nightly acts from some of the most well-known celebrities of the time — Duke Ellington, Peggy Lee, Frank Sinatra, the Marx Brothers, Bob Hope, and others.

Further down Seawall Boulevard sits Hotel Galvez, which opened in 1911, and was a popular gambling spot in the 1940s and early 1950s.

Visible from miles away, the Pleasure Pier, with its Ferris Wheel and roller coasters, was first built during World War II to entertain troops with rides, games, and an outdoor theater.

Fort Crockett Park, another reminder of war's role in the Island's history, occupies a few hundred feet of seawall with tables, benches, white canvas shade, and palm trees. Fort Crockett was home to the U.S. Army Coast Artillery troops, an artillery battery prepared for battle with German submarines in the First and Second World Wars, a World War II prisoner of war camp, and an army recreation center.

We stopped at a few of Artist Boat's concrete benches, which feature mosaic tile paintings that tell the history and depict the enviroment of Galveston. In 2016, the decorative benches were placed on the seawall in honor of local families and community members. Artist Boat is a Galveston Island-based coastal conservation and education nonprofit formed in 2003. It has conserved hundreds of acres of native habitat on the Island and actively restores and promotes green space as a necessary part of Galveston's future.

Hyacinths, a freshwater plant, covered the shoreline. The plants had washed up on the beach after the recent rains. Flooding inland carried the plants downriver, out into the Gulf, and currents

and the wind brought them ashore. We saw the plants all over the beach on Bolivar Peninsula and Galveston Island.

We've seen some areas with shells, but most of the beaches on this island are strictly sand. Stores, hotels, homes, and condos cover almost every inch of the seawall and many of the sand dunes. Those structures are often built right on the dunes or beach, just a few feet from the water, even though the beach is public.

Today was easier going than the previous days. It was cloudy, and we had the chance to stop and get on the phone with Dr. Brzeski and Dr. vonHoldt, who are studying the Island's "Ghost Wolves." In the documentary series, we are highlighting the role these coyotes with red wolf genetics play in the development and conservation of Galveston Island.

merican alligator, covered
duckweed, at Houston
udubon's Smith Oaks Bird
anctuary at High Island.

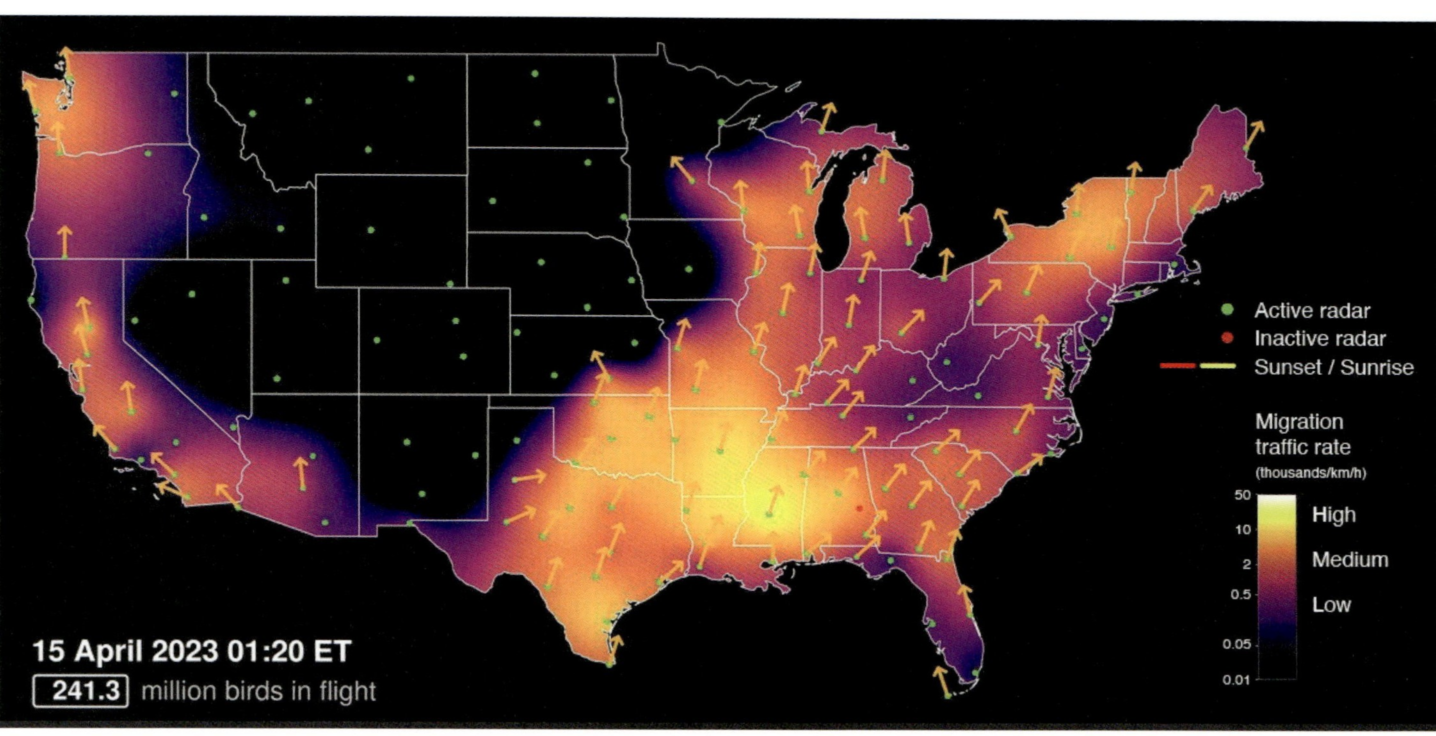

Active radar
Inactive radar
Sunset / Sunrise
Migration traffic rate
(thousands/km/h)
50
10
2
0.5
0.05
0.01
High
Medium
Low
15 April 2023 01:20 ET
241.3 million birds in flight

As I turn south from Winnie to High Island, my truck's headlights illuminate heavy sheets of rain as they hurdle through the late afternoon's fading glow. I glance at the weather radar on my phone. Shades of rain intensity—orange, yellow, and green—blanket the area between Houston and Port Arthur, and another large swath of heavy thunderstorms covers an area from the Yucatán to Atlanta.

Although High Island is but a postage stamp along Texas' 3,300 miles of estuarine coastline, its isolation amid a flat, wetland expanse makes it a mecca for bird migration. Surrounded by coastal marsh, High Island sits atop a pressurized salt dome that provides just enough reprieve from the salty soil to allow a variety of trees to grow. Houston Audubon and the Texas Ornithological Society help conserve this critical migrant stopover, not to mention colonial waterbird nesting area, which provides shelter, food, and water for songbirds as they make their biannual passage. Sites like this that concentrate larger than usual numbers of migrating birds are called migrant traps and are ideal locations for filming. These areas attract hundreds of birders from around the country and the world. The severe storms over the Gulf of Mexico tonight could force many birds migrating from the Yucatan Peninsula to the United States to stop at High Island to rest and refuel, and we plan to capture them on film.

I swipe my phone and switch to BirdCast. The tool, developed by The Cornell Lab of Ornithology, Colorado State University, and UMass Amherst, uses weather surveillance radar and modeling to predict and monitor bird migrations across the continental U.S. BirdCast's real-time map shows more than 240 million birds flying over the U.S. tonight. In Galveston County alone, more than 200,000 birds have crossed the Gulf of Mexico and are above the coastline between Galveston Island and Bolivar Peninsula. Their 18- to 24-hour, 600-mile journey across the Gulf of Mexico started as the sun set over Campeche and Cancun. During the flight, some may have encountered headwinds or rain while over the water and turned back to Mexico. Others will press on to the Gulf of Mexico's barrier islands and northern coastline. For some, the weather may have been too severe and their fat stores too low to go on, so they succumbed to exhaustion and fell into the sea.

LEFT

(Top) Great Egrets and other colonial waterbirds raise their young on High Island because of the abundant resources. (Bottom) Birdcast radar depicted more than 240 million birds in flight over the U.S. on the night before one of our film shoots at High Island.

High Island, elevated above the surrounding wetlands and on the edge of the Gulf of Mexico, provides a refuge for migrating birds.

These birds travel great distances each year between wintering sites and spring breeding grounds. Tomorrow afternoon, I will see many of them feeding on mulberries and caterpillars and bathing in one of High Island's many artificial water drips (bird baths situated on the ground and in more natural settings).

More than half of the 650-plus species of North American birds migrate. They migrate from areas where food, water, and nesting locations are dwindling to places where these resources are on the upswing. Birds that nest in the Northern Hemisphere tend to migrate northward in the spring when insects are more abundant, plants are budding, and conditions are favorable to rear young.

According to a 2019 study, an average of 2.1 billion birds cross the entire length of the Gulf Coast each spring as they head north to their breeding grounds. The study found that five times more migrant birds cross the Texas coast than any other part of the northern Gulf, with the highest rates of passage occurring between Corpus Christi and Brownsville.[1] The study proved that Texas has some of the highest recorded migratory bird passage rates in the world. Texas boasts diversity as well, with 333 of 338 species listed as neotropical migrants in North America recorded in the state. Said differently, Texas is critical to the survival of millions of migrating songbirds.

Even more impressive, Texas is only midway in their spring and fall journeys. Take the Scarlet Tanager, for instance. Some begin spring migration in late March as far south as Ecuador and reach their breeding grounds 3,500 miles away in southern Canada by early May. Months after chicks are born, they will make their way back entirely on their own to wintering grounds in Central or South America, despite having never before made the journey. Unlike waterfowl or shorebirds, they don't migrate in flocks or learn migratory patterns from their parents. They rely on a combination of genetics, the sun, stars, landmarks, a keen sense of smell, and the earth's magnetic field to navigate.

RIGHT
More than 400 bird species use the Texas coast during autumn and spring migrations. Some birds travel from as far north as the Arctic regions of Canada, and some will travel as far as the southern tip of South America.

Karine Aigner, the newest addition to our film crew, and Chrissy are here to capture the diversity of songbirds passing through the area and highlight the importance of Texas' coastal habitat to millions of birds. Chrissy met Karine a few months ago at a

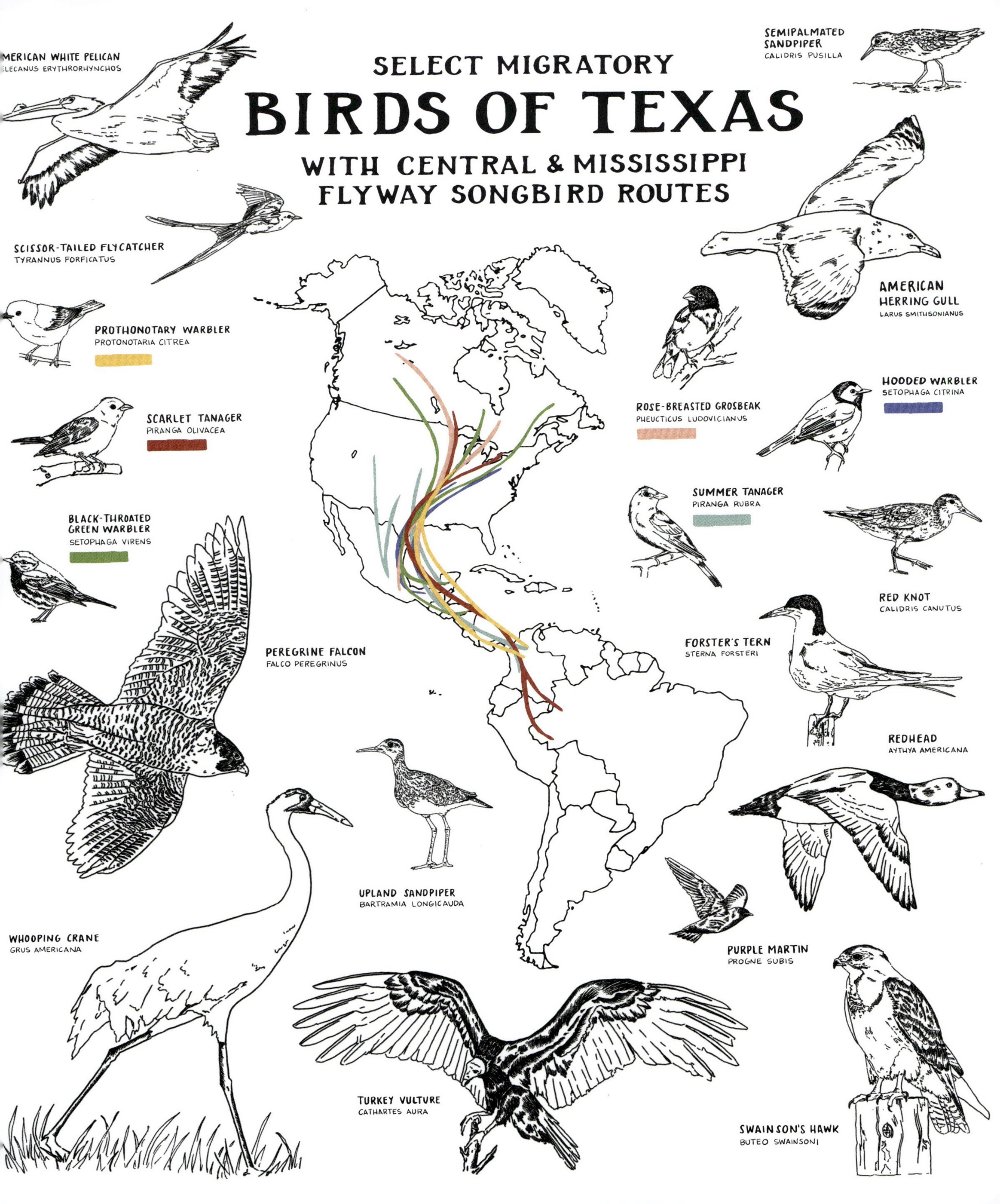
SELECT MIGRATORY
BIRDS OF TEXAS
WITH CENTRAL & MISSISSIPPI
FLYWAY SONGBIRD ROUTES
MERICAN WHITE PELICAN
ELECANUS ERYTHRORHYNCHOS
SEMIPALMATED SANDPIPER
CALIDRIS PUSILLA
SCISSOR-TAILED FLYCATCHER
TYRANNUS FORFICATUS
AMERICAN HERRING GULL
LARUS SMITHSONIANUS
PROTHONOTARY WARBLER
PROTONOTARIA CITREA
HOODED WARBLER
SETOPHAGA CITRINA
SCARLET TANAGER
PIRANGA OLIVACEA
ROSE-BREASTED GROSBEAK
PHEUCTICUS LUDOVICIANUS
SUMMER TANAGER
PIRANGA RUBRA
BLACK-THROATED GREEN WARBLER
SETOPHAGA VIRENS
RED KNOT
CALIDRIS CANUTUS
FORSTER'S TERN
STERNA FORSTERI
PEREGRINE FALCON
FALCO PEREGRINUS
REDHEAD
AYTHYA AMERICANA
UPLAND SANDPIPER
BARTRAMIA LONGICAUDA
WHOOPING CRANE
GRUS AMERICANA
PURPLE MARTIN
PROGNE SUBIS
TURKEY VULTURE
CATHARTES AURA
SWAINSON'S HAWK
BUTEO SWAINSONI

RED Camera workshop in Los Angeles. An accomplished photographer, Karine is in the early days of learning to film for documentaries.

For Chrissy and Karine, this has been a challenging shoot. The Blackburnian Warbler, Cape May, Tennessee Warbler, and other species don't sit still very long. Many of them are flitting between branches in the shadow-filled understory. To a birder, a glimpse through high-powered binoculars is enough to check off a species from the list. To our film team with heavy, immobile equipment, the die-hard birder is not always a reliable location scout.

There are several preserves on High Island, and Karine and Chrissy spend each day hopping around, like the birds they're chasing, between locations. There's a 5-acre sanctuary that was once the site of an early 20th-century hotel that local birders say is popular among some migrants because of its proximity to the ocean. There's also an old 1879 farmstead that, along with the cultivation of peaches, pears, oranges, strawberries, cabbage, sugar cane, cotton, and tobacco, was the site of a mineral water enterprise that the landowner, Mr. George Smith, trademarked and sold as "High Island Mineral Springs Water" along the Texas Gulf Coast.

In the late afternoon following the thunderstorms, some wary migrants fall into the canopy of live oak, water oak, hackberry, and ash and rest in the understory of privet, yaupon, beautyberry, English ivy, trumpet creeper, and greenbrier. Karine films a Hooded Warbler and a Blackpoll Warbler bathing in one of the drips. Chrissy posts up at a mulberry and captures several Scarlet Tanagers, Summer Tanagers, Rose-breasted Grosbeaks, Indigo Buntings, and a total of 18 different species devouring berries to replenish their energy stores before continuing their journeys in the coming days.

Before embarking on this documentary film project, most of my work on the Texas coast had been marked by human-induced disasters, such as the Deepwater Horizon oil spill, Hurricane Harvey, and rising sea levels.

LEFT
From top left to right: Rose-breasted Grosbeak, Black-throated Green Warbler, Scarlet Tanager, Indigo Bunting, and Hooded Warbler.

A Little Blue Heron nests in the dense canopy of a willow tree at High Island.

ABOVE
A Whooping Crane at Powderhorn Ranch. Photo courtesy of Jonathan Vail.

In the wake of the 2010 Deepwater Horizon explosion, which killed 11 workers and released millions of barrels of oil into the Gulf of Mexico over 87 days, Texas worked with state and federal partners to prioritize recovery efforts with more than $1 billion in expected funds through 2033. As associate director of Texas Parks and Wildlife Foundation at the time, I spent the better part of five years on a team that acquired, restored, and managed Powderhorn Ranch—one of the largest remaining undisturbed tracts of native coastal prairie habitat left in Texas. We acquired tens of thousands of acres of undeveloped Texas barrier islands and coastline habitat using the same combination of philanthropic and Deepwater Horizon settlement dollars.

After Hurricane Harvey hit the Texas coast with 3 feet of rain in late August 2017, I towed a boat behind my truck with several friends to attempt to rescue people in Houston from the floodwaters. We were just a few hours behind the Cajun Navy and other volunteers and decided to make our way across the ferry at Galveston to reach Port Arthur, which had partly been cut off from rescue by the flooding of Interstate 10. Upon reaching High Island, we were blocked by an expanse of chin-deep water

ABOVE
Hurricane Harvey hit Texas in late August 2017. Jay and friends traveled the flooded streets of Port Arthur by boat in search of survivors.

that flooded all roads leading north. We backtracked and made it to Port Arthur, but only in time to help those who had already lost everything travel from local shelters to their homes to retrieve their animals and waterlogged belongings. Harvey would be just one of five 500-year storms to hit the region between 2015 and 2019.

More recently, as the executive director of the newly established Gulf of Mexico Trust, a nonprofit organization advancing Texas-based, science-backed solutions to the Gulf of Mexico's most pressing challenges, I've spent more time studying the impacts of climate change on Texas' communities, economy, and environment.

There has already been more than 2 feet of sea level rise in Galveston in the last 100 years, while the global average during that time was about 8 inches.[2] While climate models predict that Texas could experience 1 to 4 feet of sea level rise by the end of the century as compared to the beginning, the state's shoreline could see even greater rates of sea level rise by 2100, depending on how much carbon dioxide humans pump into the atmosphere.[3] A 2009 report on the socioeconomic impacts of sea level rise in the

Galveston Bay region by the Harte Research Institute for Gulf of Mexico Studies at Texas A&M University–Corpus Christi suggested that a sea level rise of 5 feet by 2109 has the potential to displace more than 93 percent of Galveston households.[4]

What do all of these changes mean for migrating songbirds? Many of the birds we capture on camera may continue to see their populations decline. The potential for another Deepwater Horizon exists—there are more than 3,200 active oil and gas wells in the Gulf of Mexico and approximately 14,000 unplugged wells. Climate change may cause more intense storms and the loss of shoreline habitat due to sea level rise. According to a study published in *Science* in September 2019, the number of North American migrating birds between 2007 and 2017 dropped by about 14 percent. Overall, bird populations in the United States and Canada have declined by 29 percent between 1970 and 2017, representing a loss of almost three billion birds.[5]

RIGHT
An Indigo Bunting rests before resuming its journey north for the summer.

In many places, the spring thaw arrives earlier and earlier, causing insects to emerge sooner and late-arriving migrants to miss opportunities to feed themselves and their young. Climate change will also lead to longer migrations as summer breeding grounds shift north with warming temperatures. Longer migrations mean birds will increasingly rely on refueling stopovers like High Island, making it and other areas like it essential.

CHAPTER 3

GHOST WOLVES

HIDING IN PLAIN SIGHT

Day: 6
Miles walked: 108
Miles remaining: 262

October 6, 2023

We made the call late last night to pick up the mileage between High Island and Sea Rim State Park since we had to leapfrog to Bolivar Peninsula on October 2nd due to lack of support on McFaddin Beach.

On the evening of the 5th, we drove from Surfside Beach, having jogged into the night to get there, crossed by ferry from Galveston to Bolivar Peninsula, then finally arrived at our rent house by 9:30 p.m. The film crew geared up for the next day. John Aldrich would shoot with Patrick Thrash in the morning and then switch out with Henry Davis. Patrick and Henry would hitch a ride and meet us midday halfway down McFaddin Beach.

We also had construction on 20 miles of beach ahead of us. We have a short window of time to complete this section, as McFaddin Beach is getting a makeover. For now, though, the restoration is at a standstill. The dredge used to bring sand offshore to the beach is undergoing maintenance. Once it's back in service in a few weeks, the U.S. Fish and Wildlife Service, U.S. Army Corps of Engineers, and the Texas General Land Office won't let anyone on the beach. If we don't walk it now, we may have to wait until spring. At that point, temperatures will start rising again.

We started early on the 5th and departed High Island, where Highway 87 had been lost to the sea, at sunrise. That road once connected Bolivar Peninsula to Sabine Pass. After several hurricanes and rising sea levels, it remains underwater.

We'd heard that a section halfway between High Island and Sea Rim State Park was impassable. Terry Harris, a local hunting guide, offered to provide us with support and give our camera crew a ride down the beach.

Terry was a longtime friend of Ellis Pickett, who joined us a couple of days ago. We met Ellis a few months

while filming in Port Arthur and Galveston. Gene Gore, whom we met while filming Kemp's ridley sea turtles on South Padre Island in June 2023, suggested that we connect with Ellis. Gene is a South Padre surf instructor. Our friends at Sea Turtle, Inc., whom we filmed relocating and releasing juvenile Kemp's ridleys, introduced us to Gene.

Ellis had provided logistical support to Gene and his wife, Rachel, in 2004 when the Goves paddleboarded the entire length of the Texas coast. A shark struck Rachel's board and tossed into the water on their first day. She got back on her board and completed the trip from the Rio Grande to the Sabine River in 19 days. Rachel's story put the challenges of our first day into perspective.

Ellis Pickett founded the first Surfrider Foundation chapter in Texas. He has been surfing for several decades and been an advocate for beach access for the past twenty years. He has accompanied us since we hit Bolivar Peninsula and is providing us with information and connections that are proving to be invaluable. He found Terry for us, called elected officials in Galveston to grant us access to a closed park, and is applying a lifetime of experience on the Texas coast to benefit this project.

When we had walked about 10 miles that day, we came to a half-mile section of hard, black clay with holes and ridges that spread out into the ocean like fingers. Water surged over the holes and deposited seashells, with and without inhabitants.

Terry wanted to see his grandson play high school football in nearby Winnie that night, so he left with the film crew for the 10-mile drive back to where we started. A few miles after crossing the clay and shell section, we met up again with Ellis, who had driven 80 miles from High Island to Port Arthur and McFaddin Beach to reach us.

The walking was easy in most sections near the shore. The beach was made of fine brown sand with ridges of clay that looked like sandstone in some places and, in other places, looked like black volcanic rock.

To the touch, some of this clay was soft and melted in our hands. Parts of the clay in some sections of the beach had broken off and been tumbled by the fluctuating tides and unrelenting waves to the point that there were perfectly round spheres and conical shapes made of sand and mud holding shell and rock fragments.

We passed some of the metal pipes used to bring dredged sand from roughly a mile offshore. The Texas General Land Office and partners were bringing the sand through a large pipe and spreading it along the first two hundred yards or so of beach and on top of that clay layer. Up from the new sandy beach, they've also created an artificial dune system that runs paralell to the shoreline and stands about 10 feet or more above sea level.

When completed, the new beach and dunes will protect about 20 miles of beach and the wetlands behind. Towards the day's final stretch, we encountered some old oil and gas equipment built on top of a salt dome. We rested there before setting off on the last 5 miles. Further down the beach, we found a dead dolphin that looked like it had died from natural causes — no bite marks or prop scars — and we notified the Texas Marine Mammal Stranding Network.

We hiked 23 hard miles today. At about mile 15, our bodies started hurting. Our feet, knees, and legs ached from so many hours of walking. Fortunately, we had support from Terry, who made it to his grandson's football game in Winnie. We ended the day in Sabine Pass, had a pepperoni pizza and two Big Reds at the gas station, and then drove three hours back to Surfside Beach to pick up where we left off.

On the drive, Ellis talked about surfing oil tanker wakes off of Galveston Island while Chrissy and I silently processed the junk food and the day. We had walked 23 miles in 12 hours. The weight of completing the McFaddin Beach section we had missed on the first days of the walk was finally off our backs.

SEA WALL GRADE RAISING
STARTED DEC. 12TH 1903.
FINISHED FEB. 16TH 1911.
SEA WALL BOULEVARD AND SIDEWALK
STARTED FEB. 15TH 1906,
FINISHED FEB. 28TH 1912.
COUNTY JUDGE, GEO. E. MANN.
COUNTY COMMISSIONERS,
ALEX. GOMEZ, FIRST PRECINCT.
FRED. C. PABST, SECOND PRECINCT,
R. W. WOLSTON, THIRD PRECINCT,
H. A. DEATS, FOURTH PRECINCT.
COUNTY CLERK, COUNTY AUDITOR,
GEO. F. BURGESS. JOHN M. MURCH.
COUNTY ENGINEER, ASST. CO. ENGINEER,
H. M. SIAS. C. A. HOLT, JR.
GALVESTON SEA WALL
CONSTRUCTED UNDER THE FOLLOWING
COUNTY OFFICIALS.
JUDGE
LEWIS FISHER,
CLERK
GEO. H. LAW JR.
COMMISSIONERS
J. M. O. MENARD, R. W. WOLSTON,
D. B. HENDERSON, T. J. DICK,
J. T. WHEELER, Co. ATTY.
W. CAMPBELL, Co. JUDGE 1901-2.

SEA WALL
AND GRADE ELEVATION.
DESIGNED BY
GEN'L. H. M. ROBERT,
ALFRED NOBLE,
H. C. RIPLEY,
ENGINEERS.
GALVESTON SEA WALL
CONSTRUCTION
COMMENCED OCT. 27TH 1902.
COMPLETED JULY 30TH 1904.
GEO. W. BOSCHKE,
ENGINEER.
JOHN M. O'ROURKE.
GEO. N. STEINMETZ.
CONTRACTORS.
24

Against all odds, including a government-sanctioned trapping program and an increasingly industrialized and populated Gulf Coast, the Ghost Wolves of Galveston Island and their red wolf genetics have persisted. For several decades now, they have been roaming unnoticed in the remnant prairies, lagoons, and streets of this barrier island. The markings of their red wolf ancestors—large bodies, broad heads, long legs, and fur with a distinctively reddish hue—are unfamiliar to us today, having been hunted and trapped out of existence decades ago.

The canines of Galveston Island—part red wolf, part coyote—have found a home on a barrier island with more than 50,000 residents and 6.5 million visitors annually. They range as far as 100 miles down the coast and utilize pockets of open space to hunt and raise their young. This story is important not only because it highlights a wildlife species' survival against the odds, but also because of the role this island and its human inhabitants play in the fight for the Ghost Wolves' future.

To understand these animals, we must rewind the clock to a time before European arrival in North America. Gray wolves ranged across much of the continent, and coyotes inhabited the West. Although each has distinct characteristics and behaviors, recent genetic research suggests that these two lineages diverged from a common ancestor between six thousand and 117 thousand years ago.[1]

The red wolf may not even be considered a unique wolf species. The same team of scientists led by Dr. Bridgett vonHoldt—an evolutionary biologist at Princeton University—that closely linked gray wolves and coyotes found that red wolves are highly admixed, or hybridized, with different proportions of gray wolf and coyote ancestry.[2] Wolves began disappearing from the landscape as early Europeans settled the American South and East, converting woodland habitat to agricultural landscape. Then, in the 1880s, private, state, and federal bounty programs targeted wolves, eliminating them from the southeastern landscape. As wolves became scarce and coyotes moved east toward more suitable habitats, it became increasingly difficult for wolves to find mates from the same species, increasing coyote-wolf hybridization. The red wolf is emblematic of human-induced stressors and genetic adaptability.

RIGHT
A Ghost Wolf on Galveston Island's East End.

GHOST WOLVES OF GALVESTON ISLAND

THE RED WOLF IS THE MOST ENDANGERED WOLF IN THE WORLD. SCIENTISTS HAVE IDENTIFIED CANINE POPULATIONS ALONG THE GULF COAST THAT ARE RESERVOIRS OF UNIQUE RED WOLF GENES ONCE BELIEVED TO BE EXTINCT. THE GALVESTON ISLAND GHOST WOLVES ARE NAMED FOR THESE "GHOST" GENES AND REPRESENT A ONE-OF-A-KIND POPULATION THAT MAY BEHAVE AND RESPOND TO ENVIRONMENTAL CHANGE DIFFERENTLY THAN OTHER CANINES. BASING CONSERVATION WORK ON AN ANIMAL'S APPEARANCE ALONE CAN BE PROBLEMATIC, BUT THESE UNIQUE TEXAS CANINES LOOK MARKEDLY DIFFERENT FROM THE COMMON COYOTE.

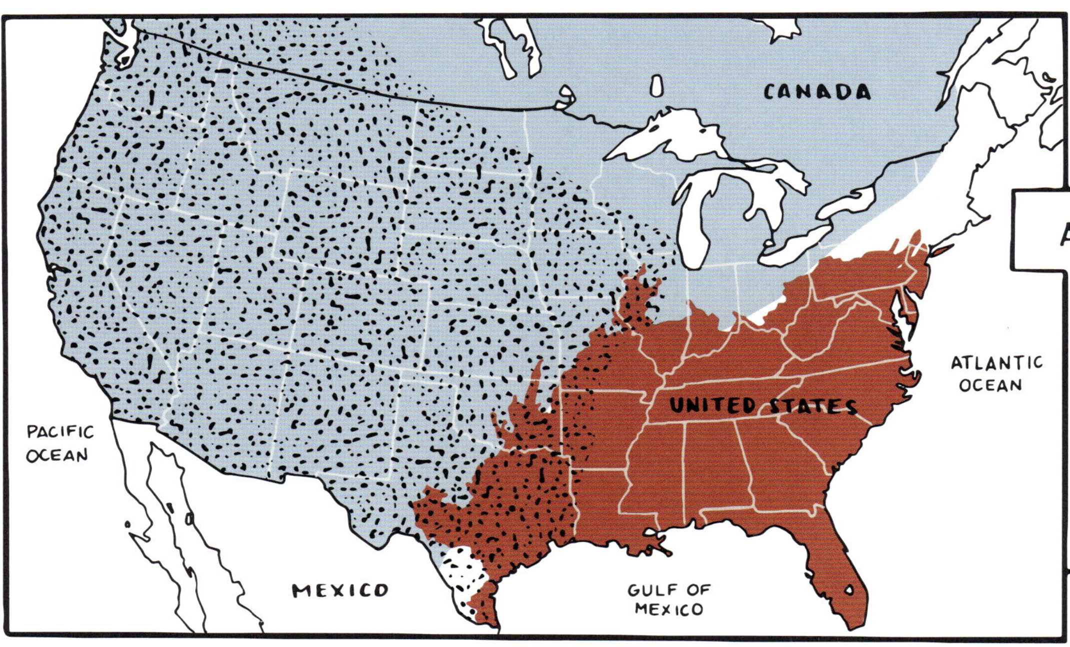

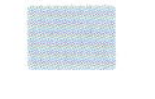 HISTORIC RANGE OF THE GRAY WOLF

 HISTORIC RANGE OF THE THE RED WOLF

 HISTORIC RANGE OF COYOTES

SOURCES: A CUADRA / SCIENCE, AAAS
NATIONAL GEOGRAPHIC. C

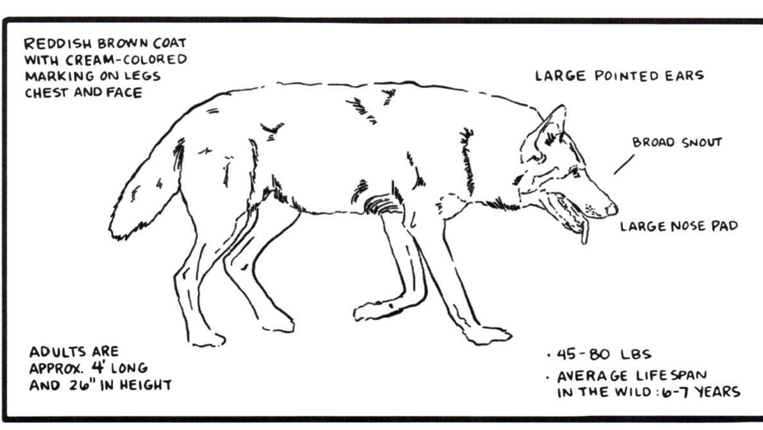

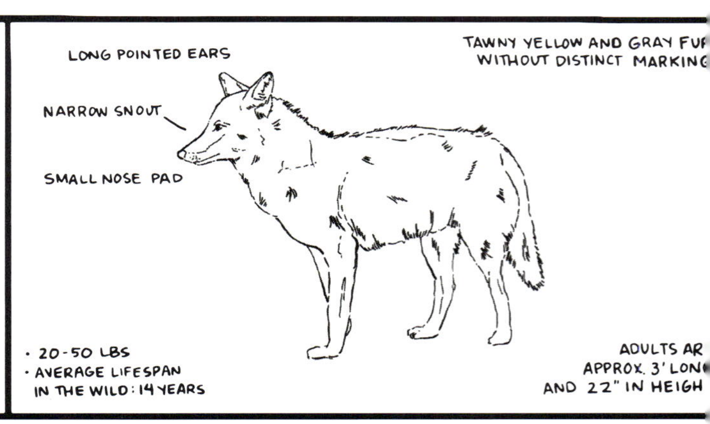

RED WOLF

CANIS RUFUS

CRITICALLY ENDANGERED - ESTIMATED LESS THAN 40

- DECLARED EXTINCT IN THE WILD IN 1980 (U.S.A.) DUE TO HABITAT LOSS, COYOTE INTERBREEDING, PREDATOR CONTROL PROGRAMS, AND DISEASE.
- REINTRODUCED IN NORTH CAROLINA FROM CAPTIVE BREEDING PROGRAM WITH A SMALL POPULATION IN 1987.

COYOTE

CANIS LATRANS

CLASSIFIED AS A LEAST-CONCERN SPECIES

- MODERN COYOTES HAVE ADAPTED TO THE CHANGING LANDSCAPE WITH BOTH URBAN AND RURAL COLONIES.
- THE COYOTE POPULATIONS ARE LIKELY AT AN ALL-TIME HIGH.

In the 1960s, red wolf populations suffered severe declines due to intensive government-led predator control initiatives and habitat loss. In 1962, Howard McCarley, a professor at Austin College, suggested that a significant portion of the animals commonly perceived as red wolves were, in fact, hybrids of wolves and coyotes. The red wolf population was declining more quickly than expected. A 1974 edition of *The Mammals of Texas* states, "All of the recent, so-called red wolves I have examined from eastern Texas have proven to be large coyotes. Consequently, it appears that in Texas, red wolves are now restricted to the Gulf Coast counties and are on the verge of extinction."[3]

A small group of red wolves did manage to survive along the Gulf Coast of Texas and Louisiana. Recognizing their endangered status, the United States Fish and Wildlife Service (USFWS) launched an ambitious program in 1973 to locate and capture the remaining wild red wolves, establish a captive breeding program, and someday establish a wild population again. Biologists successfully captured approximately 400 canids, of which more than 40 were thought to be red wolves, and moved them to Point Defiance Zoo and Aquarium in Tacoma, Washington. Eventually, only 14 individuals were successfully bred and became the founders of today's red wolf. In 1980, USFWS officially declared the red wolf extinct in their natural habitat.

USFWS was ultimately successful in its efforts to build a captive breeding population, and in 1987 a reintroduction program began in northeastern North Carolina. By 2010, approximately 130 wild red wolves roamed 1.7 million acres of public and private land in northeast North Carolina. Then, in 2011 and 2012, a combination of factors once again caused the population to plummet—vehicle strikes, hunters mistaking the wolves for coyotes, and targeted poaching associated with a misinformation campaign about red wolves. As of early 2023, 14 known red wolves were in the wild in North Carolina's Albemarle Peninsula.

While the descendants of the government's recovery program struggle to survive on the Atlantic Coast, the genetics of their ancestors endure in the Ghost Wolf population on the Texas and Louisiana Gulf Coast. Researchers have recently begun to unravel clues about red wolves who evaded trapping efforts in the 1970s and bred with local coyotes. Drs. Kristin Brzeski and Bridgett vonHoldt established the Gulf Coast Canine Project after their initial

ABOVE
Drs. Kristin Brzeski and Bridgett vonHoldt during an interview on Galveston Island.

canine research on Galveston Island uncovered the prevalence of rare red wolf genetic variants, or "ghost alleles," that researchers thought had gone extinct.[4]

According to Dr. vonHoldt, "So the ghost part [of the name 'Ghost Wolves'] is in reference to the extinction of red wolves. We presumed they took all of their genes with them. But what we also have to remember is when a population is dying out, it might find the best mate is the next closest related species. So, a red wolf and a coyote can have offspring. Maybe the red wolf dies because that's what's been happening for red wolves, but all of those genes that it just passed on to its coyote hybrid offspring now get to circulate, and we've rediscovered those."

To get background information before our attempt to film the Ghost Wolves on Galveston Island, we reached out to Ron Wooten. A public affairs specialist for the U.S. Army Corps of Engineers and an amateur wildlife photographer, he began taking notice of the unusual-looking coyotes on the island in 2008. Ten years later, with tissue samples from a road kill and the help of Drs. vonHoldt and Brzeski, Wooten's hunch proved positive—the canines they tested were half red wolf and half coyote.

ABOVE
We stopped on Galveston Island to talk with Ron Wooten, whose interest in the island's coyotes sparked efforts to study and protect their habitat.

Our phone conversation focused on the logistics of finding and filming the animals over five days in the coming months. It will be spring breeding season, and the Ghost Wolves will be active, but we would also be facing long odds of capturing them on camera. Even with GPS collars on two of the Ghost Wolves and a community map that has tracked more than 100 coyote sightings since 2021, we'll be guessing where an elusive predator will be on an island half the size of Dallas. Ron's list of potential shoot locations runs the entire 27 miles of Galveston Island. It highlights the odd mix of open space and built environment these animals occupy—Jamaica Beach, Galveston Island State Park, East End Lagoon, Artist Boat's Coastal Heritage Preserve, Moody Gardens Convention Center, the airport, and the Randalls grocery store parking lot.

Ron suggested that we speak directly with Drs. Brzeski and vonHoldt to get an update on their research, so we scheduled a call a few weeks later. To prepare for that conversation, I did some research of my own and found a *Scientific American* interview with the scientists. In the interview, the two researchers discussed the significance of their findings—not only that these canine populations along the Gulf Coast could be reservoirs of unique red wolf genes once believed to be extinct, but also that the Galveston Ghost Wolves represent a one-of-a-kind population that may behave and respond to environmental change differently than other canines.

A Ghost Wolf braves the surf on the Galveston shoreline. Photo courtesy of Ron Wooten.

Somehow, rather than being diluted by coyote genes, the red wolf genes survived in high percentages. It opened up new possibilities in endangered species recovery efforts. Dr. vonHoldt described what it might mean to introduce the current population of red wolves with the admixed canids, or Ghost Wolves, found in Texas and Louisiana: "This would be kind of the opposite direction, taking the small isolated, you know, inbred population from the captive breeding program that still has red wolf genes that are so critical, and put them into a wild landscape with new genetic variation that they haven't seen for 50 years or more. And all of a sudden, hopefully, this is like a super mix of genetic health and sort of a rebound that these animals can be wild and be themselves again."[5] In other words, we could turn back the clock before the genetic bottleneck in 1980 and support a more genetically diverse red wolf population.

Over the phone, we discussed the red wolf's history as well as the researchers' work in Texas and Louisiana. They suggested that beyond these scientific discoveries, their work has uncovered new ways of looking at the community's role in wildlife conservation and mixed ancestry in species recovery. These animals, previously considered run-of-the-mill coyotes, are thriving and live alongside the people of Galveston. The Ghost Wolves have survived hurricanes, development, and a statewide culture that continues to hunt these predators largely because community members have embraced them. These canids have brought national attention to Galveston, in large part because of a 2022 article in *The New York Times*, and are considered unique to the region, resulting in a community effort to monitor, research, and protect their habitat.

Basing conservation work on an animal's appearance, or phenotype, can be deceiving. There's considerable variation in the way coyotes look, which is why they're doing genetic work to identify the extent to which these wolf/coyote hybrids exist. Historically, USFWS has excluded wildlife species from conservation protection that do not conform to an observable physical standard. Using the Ghost Wolf as an example, the researchers suggest that this traditional way of thinking about species conservation may cause major oversights or exclusion of critical genomic variation potentially useful for genomic rescue or local adaptation through targeted practices. As technology continues to provide innovative methods, the Gulf Coast canids also represent a critical biobanking opportunity when

LEFT
(Top) A Ghost Wolf peers back at the camera on Artist Boat's Coastal Heritage Preserve on Galveston Island.
(Bottom) East End Lagoon Preserve on Galveston Island provides cover for this Ghost Wolf.

ABOVE
This pack of Ghost Wolves weaves through a mixture of habitat and busy streets on Galveston Island.

RIGHT
Galveston Island's Pleasure Pier rises above the mist.

genome editing methods are applied to red wolves. One of the key lessons here is, as Drs. Brzeski and vonHoldt state on their Gulf Coast Canine Project website, "Hybridization was once thought to be the greatest conservation threat to the red wolf, but now historic hybridization may be key to their recovery."

They suggested that this wildlife survival story might be similar to our own, as humans have ancestry from different regions of the globe and have adapted to their environment over millennia. Just as humans now face the challenge of adapting to climate change, scientists and officials might refocus red wolf conservation programs on areas where red wolf genes have endured amid ecological upheaval.

Chrissy, Karine Aigner, Ellen Burris, Henry Davis, and Patrick Thrash spent a week roaming Galveston Island, navigating spring break traffic and chasing leads from locals. They combed the beaches, lagoons, and parking lots in search of wild canids. Finally, Henry captured a pack on film between the 17-foot seawall and a beach hotel on the island's East End. In the background, cars and trucks meandered down a road to the beach while joggers crept along Seawall Boulevard, unaware of the Ghost Wolves hiding in plain sight.

CHAPTER 4

OUR BARRIER ISLANDS

ON THE FRONTLINE OF CHANGE

Day: 8
Miles walked: 144
Miles remaining: 226

October 8, 2023

Yesterday morning, we started in Surfside Beach, at the western end of Follet's Island. We met up with Michelle Booth, the Tourism Specialist for the Village of Surfside Beach. She and her husband, Rob, moved to Surfside in 2014, and in addition to her work to draw people to town, she leads a year-round trash cleanup initiative. She, her husband, and the local cleanup crew walked with us down the beach to the jetties on the edge of town.

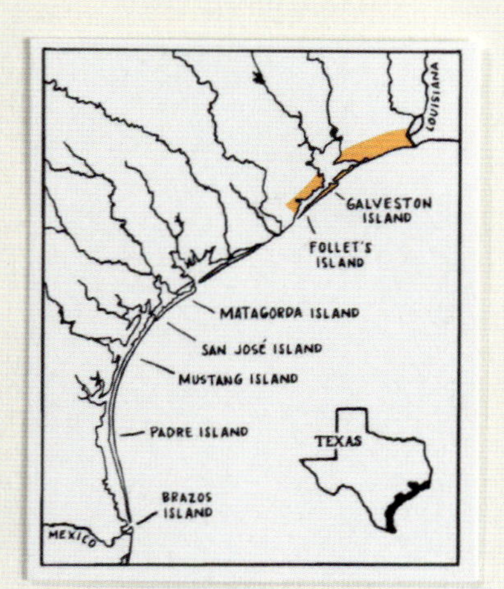

Michelle alerted the mayor, Greg Bisso, that we were coming, which gave him time to put on flip-flops, shorts, and a short-sleeve collared shirt emblazoned with the official village emblem. He greeted us outside of his house, where we chatted briefly. Mayor Bisso recounted some interesting facts about Surfside, which was the home of Fort Velasco. Stephen F. Austin

and his colonists arrived in this particular part of Texas in 1821, and in 1832, it was here that Texas fought the first battle of its war for independence.

We also met Michael, who lives in a row of a-frame houses on stilts that, as he jokingly puts it, sit in "international waters" (the Gulf of Mexico) and not the beach when the tide is high. He has a band, whose members also live in the row of a-frames. Michael invited us to their annual Surfside Beach music festival, hosted from the porch of the aforementioned stilt homes.

After meeting the mayor and Michael, two men stopped us in their pickup truck, prayed for us, drove off, and promptly returned with breakfast tacos and a plastic Buc-ees medallion—the combination of which was meant to bring us luck.

Shortly after saying goodbye to our new friends in Surfside, we got a ride from our crew around Quintana Beach and passed the Freeport Liquid Natural Gas plant. According to the locals, the company that runs the LNG plant bought most of the homes on the island, which was sandwiched between the mouth of the old Brazos River and a new channel cut by the U.S. Army Corps of Engineers in 1929. Quintana was another first for us — an actual "company island" on the Texas coast.

After walking down the beach a few miles, we made it to the new mouth of the Brazos River, where we saw Ellis Pickett on his paddleboard. He was on his knees, halfway across the river, with a half dozen anglers screaming at him. They were yelling profanities, telling him that he was going to drown and that they wouldn't save his ass if he did.

Ellis is hard of hearing and either couldn't understand why they were so excited or was simply ignoring them. Meanwhile, our crew stood calmly by, filming the whole scene. After the crowd that had now gathered coaxed him to turn back, he finally paddled back to shore and said that he was just testing the waters to see if we could make it across in our inflatable kayaks.

As Ellis pulled his board onto the beach, we spoke with one of the anglers, Victor Cruz from Rio Grande City. He explained that with the recent rains, the mix of outgoing flow from the river and incoming tide was too strong for anyone to attempt paddling across. He then added that they had recently rescued several people from near drowning and weren't in the mood to do it again.

With that in mind, we asked Victor and some others about getting a boat to ferry us across. Victor started to call a friend from nearby Freeport to bring his boat to the mouth of the river when we noticed a man casting his net off the front of his fishing boat a few hundred yards away. Victor drove me over to the man, and then he waded into the water to talk to him. The man was understandably apprehensive, having seen the drama unfold with Ellis. Victor explained that we just needed a short boat ride to continue our walk down the coast, and he thankfully offered to give us a lift.

We thanked everyone and said goodbye to our crew. Then, we finally crossed the Brazos and landed on a stretch of beach formed by the deltas, or river mouths, of the Brazos, San Bernard, and Colorado Rivers. It was a magnificent, secluded beach strewn with black, striped, and dark blue shells. There were alot of shorebirds, including Spotted Sandpipers, Semipalmated Plovers, and Willets. The most striking thing about the first mile of that shoreline was the sight of hundreds of dead, giant trees laid upon their sides — decades of trees uprooted from the banks of rivers by floods, flushed out to sea, and brought back to shore by wind, waves, and the tide.

We reached the East San Bernard River, or what remained of it, four miles from the Brazos River. It had mostly silted in, and rather than wade across, we got a lift on the tailgate of someone's truck.

Before reaching Sargent, the Jeep Club of Sargent, which also doubles as the rescue and recovery volunteer team, came out to meet us. A few of their members had been following us on social media and messaging with Chrissy about our whereabouts. They asked how we planned to make it across the next river passage at Mitchell's Cut, and when we told them that we hadn't figured that out, they offered to call a few friends and arrange a ride for us the next day.

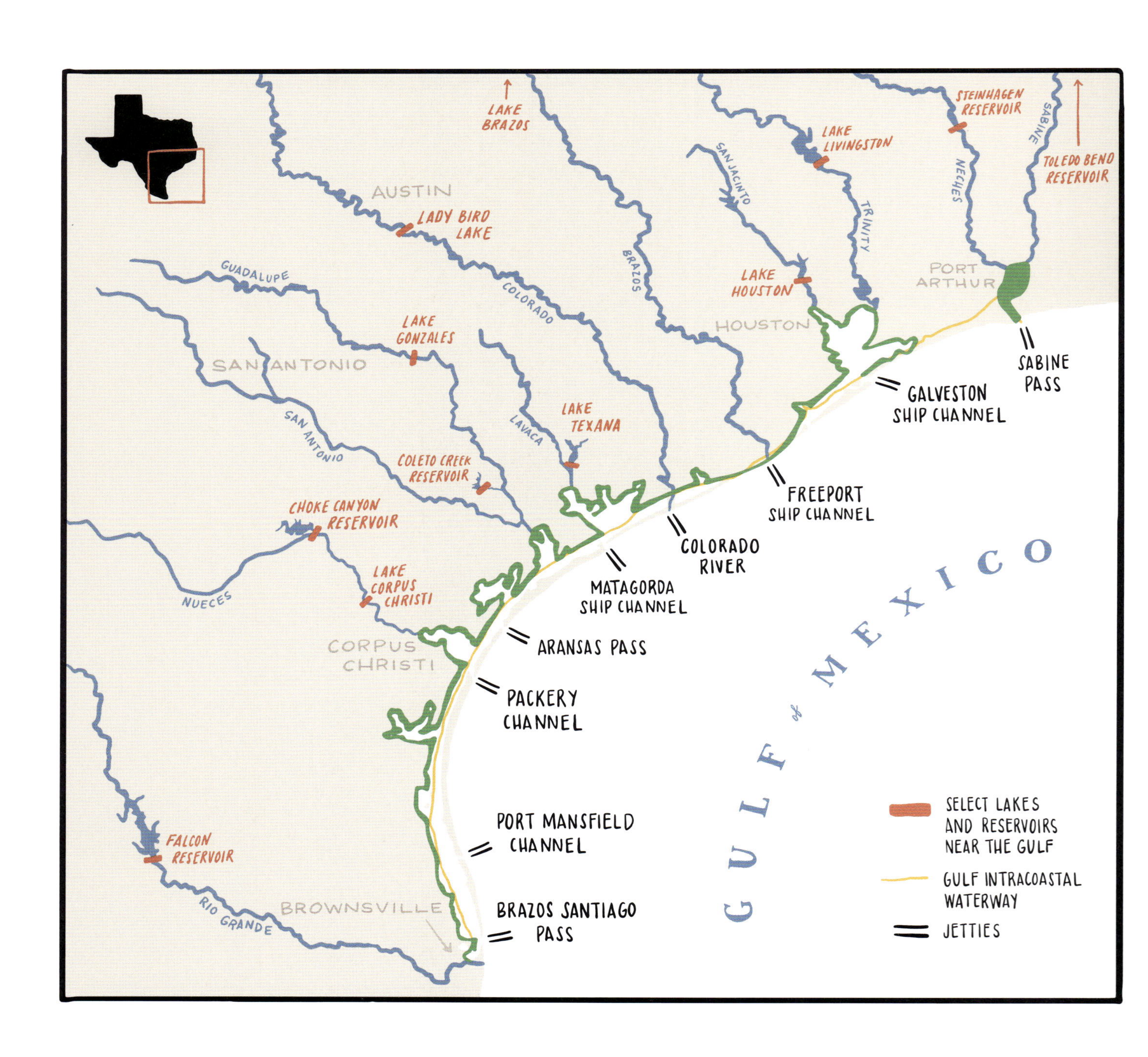

LAKE BRAZOS
STEINHAGEN RESERVOIR
SABINE
TOLEDO BEND RESERVOIR
LAKE LIVINGSTON
SAN JACINTO
NECHES
TRINITY
AUSTIN
LADY BIRD LAKE
GUADALUPE
COLORADO
BRAZOS
LAKE HOUSTON
PORT ARTHUR
HOUSTON
LAKE GONZALES
SAN ANTONIO
SAN ANTONIO
LAVACA
LAKE TEXANA
SABINE PASS
GALVESTON SHIP CHANNEL
COLETO CREEK RESERVOIR
FREEPORT SHIP CHANNEL
CHOKE CANYON RESERVOIR
COLORADO RIVER
MATAGORDA SHIP CHANNEL
LAKE CORPUS CHRISTI
NUECES
ARANSAS PASS
CORPUS CHRISTI
PACKERY CHANNEL
GULF of MEXICO
PORT MANSFIELD CHANNEL
FALCON RESERVOIR
SELECT LAKES AND RESERVOIRS NEAR THE GULF
GULF INTRACOASTAL WATERWAY
BROWNSVILLE
RIO GRANDE
BRAZOS SANTIAGO PASS
JETTIES

Texas' barrier islands began forming about 5,000 years ago. They are young by geological and human standards. Generations of early Indigenous people would have witnessed the sea rise, inundating ancient river valleys, and new land emerge from submerged sandbars. Compared to Texas' tallest peak in the Guadalupe Mountains, part of the Capitán Reef that formed at the margins of a shallow sea 250 million years ago, the barrier islands are among the state's newest features.

About 26,000 years ago, the shoreline of the Gulf of Mexico was about 400 feet lower than today. Rivers draining Texas carried sediments across the continental shelf and deposited them in Gulf of Mexico waters that would have been 100 miles east of their present position. The early makings of what would become the Trinity, Brazos, and Colorado rivers scoured deep valleys across the Coastal Plain and deposited sediment across a shallow system of river deltas. At the conclusion of the Holocene epoch, approximately 4,500 years ago, sea levels had risen to within about 15 feet of their present levels. These final sea level changes were influenced by a combination of factors, including sediment compaction, Gulf Coast region subsidence (the gradual sinking of the land), and minor glacial activity fluctuations. Parts of the old river valleys and deltas flooded and became our modern-day bays and estuaries.

When sea levels stabilized near their present-day levels several millennia ago, sand shoals formed just off the coast began joining. The previously submerged river delta and ancient barrier island sediment, deposited farther out to sea during periods of lower sea levels, provided a source for the islands to emerge from the shallow coastal waters. Waves and currents transported sand toward the shoreline, and sandbars gradually grew and evolved into a chain of short barrier islands. These first islands were predominantly situated along the breaks between river valleys, enabling an exchange of water and life in bays and estuaries protected by a series of barrier islands.

Longshore drift, currents that run parallel to the coast, deposited sand on the southern tips of the barrier islands while constantly moving water through tidal inlets eroded the northern ends. Over time, the rate of sand accumulation, or accretion, overcame many of the natural passages, and a series of long islands formed into the seven barrier islands along Texas' present-day coastline.

LEFT
By damming rivers, dredging the Gulf Intracoastal Waterway, and creating hardened jetties, Texas has altered the flow of freshwater, nutrients, and sediment to the bays, estuaries, and Gulf of Mexico.

ABOVE
These dunes and beach are part of Padre Island, the world's longest barrier island.

RIGHT
The Texas coast is experiencing some of the highest rates of sea level rise on the planet, which increases the negative impacts of flooding and storm surge on natural and human environments.

The newly joined barrier islands underwent a dual construction process—primarily vertical growth, driven by wind, and a gradual expansion toward the Gulf caused by wave action and tides. Sand transported from the continental shelf contributed to the accumulation of sand along the island shorelines. The islands also grew toward the mainland as storms and wind drove sediment over the Gulf-facing beaches and dunes. After the present-day barrier islands took shape, wind, waves, and currents continued to build, break down, and transform them.

Today, the barrier islands, like most of the Texas coast, are in a state of retreat. Beginning in the late 1800s, Texas' coastal cities and towns dredged ship channels to allow for the passage of people and goods. The U.S. Army Corps of Engineers constructed jetties using granite blocks the size of small cars to keep channels cut between and through barrier islands from silting in. Some stretch more than six miles offshore and trap sand transported up and down the coast by currents. The jetties starve the state's shoreline of sediment and weaken an important line of defense against erosion, sea level rise, and storms.

Texas also dammed all of its major rivers, first in the 1930s to control flooding and then quickening in pace after a nearly decade-long drought in the 1950s. Rivers naturally carry fresh water, sediment, and nutrients, and dams prevent these building blocks of healthy

SEA LEVEL RISE

BY 2050 LARGE SECTIONS OF THE BEACHES, ESPECIALLY ON THE UPPER COAST, ARE PROJECTED TO BE UNDERWATER. RECORDS FROM TIDAL GAUGES SHOW THAT THE SEA LEVEL ALONG THE TEXAS COAST IS RISING FASTER THAN IT HAS AT ANY POINT IN THE LAST 3000 YEARS.

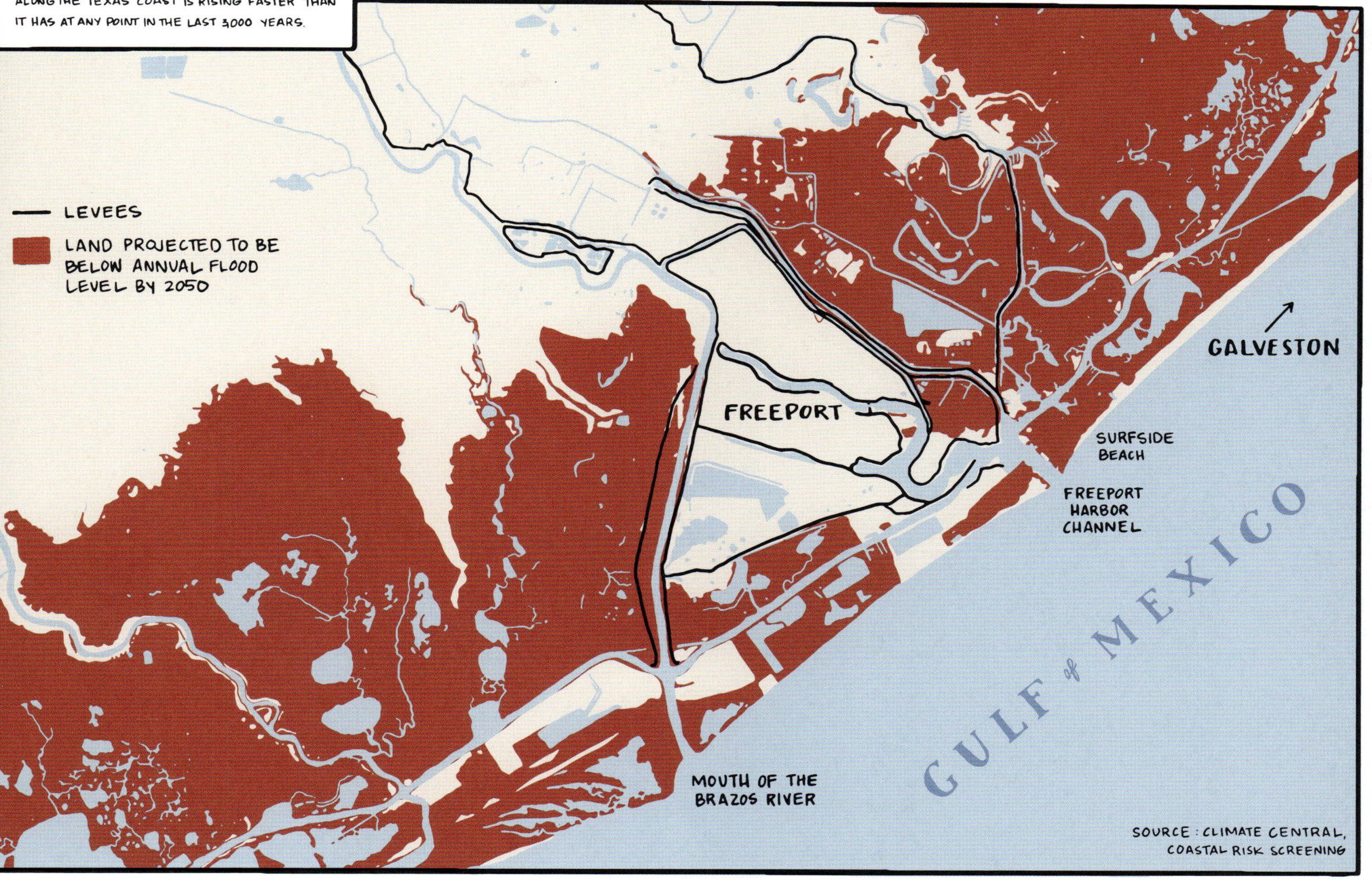

RRENT AND FUTURE RISING SEA LEVELS SIGNIFICANTLY ELEVATE THE RISK AND DAMAGE TO CRITICAL INFRASTRUCTURE AND THE SEVERITY URRICANES ALONG THE TEXAS COASTLINE. ELEVATED SEA LEVELS ALSO CAUSE THE EROSION OF COASTAL HABITAT, SUBMERGING BOTH TIDAL WETLANDS AND BARRIER ISLANDS, AFFECTING Y SPECIES OF BIRDS AND FISH, AND REMOVING NATURAL BARRIERS TO COASTAL FLOODING.

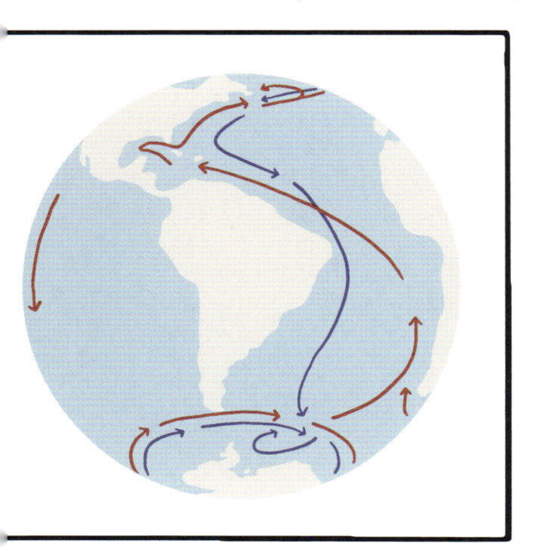

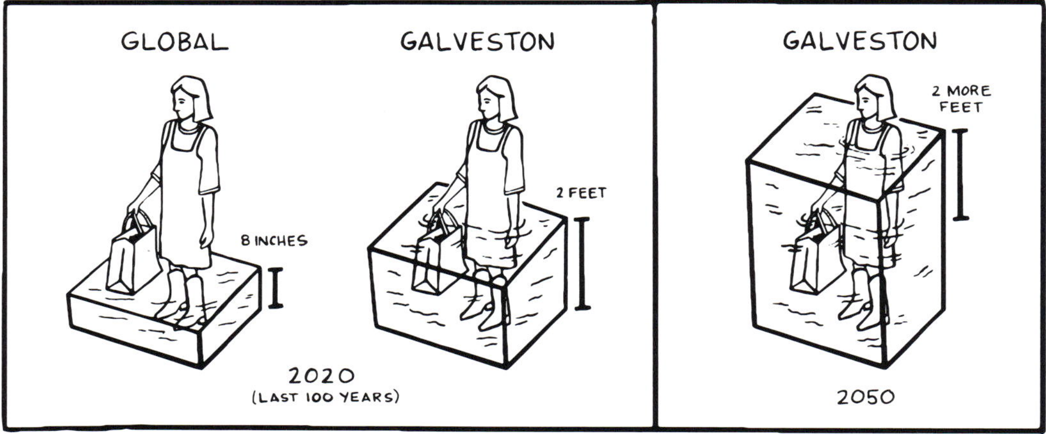

MELTING ICE IN WEST ANTARCTICA ISPROPORTIONATELY AFFECTS TEXAS IN ART BECAUSE THEY ARE CONNECTED BY AJOR OCEAN CURRENTS. SOURCE→

THERE HAS BEEN MORE THAN 2 FEET OF SEA LEVEL RISE IN GALVESTON IN THE LAST 100 YEARS, WHILE THE GLOBAL AVERAGE DURING THAT TIME WAS ABOUT 8 INCHES OF SEA RISE. GALVESTON IS EXPECTED TO EXPERIENCE ANOTHER 2 FOOT RISE BY 2050. SOURCE: RYAN KELLMAN AND REBECCA HERSHER; *WHY TEXANS NEED TO KNOW HOW FAST ANTARCTICA IS MELTING*. NATIONAL PUBLIC RADIO, APRIL 19, 2023.

ABOVE
A ship travels north on the Gulf Intracoastal Waterway near Sargent.

coastal environments from reaching estuaries, bays, beaches, and barrier islands. Without new supplies of sediment from Texas' rivers and jetties blocking sand from naturally accumulating on islands, the barrier islands no longer expand as they have for thousands of years.

The Gulf Intracoastal Waterway (GIWW), built during the first part of the 20th century, cuts through the shallow bays and behind the islands and, in Texas, stretches 426 miles from Sabine Pass to the mouth of the Brownsville Ship Channel at Port Isabel. The GIWW sliced through and damaged some wetlands, cutting off life-giving freshwater flow to some areas and allowing salt water to kill salt-intolerant plants in others. The loss of wetlands meant that barrier islands were even more exposed to erosion and the coast was losing critical nursery grounds for fish and other wildlife.

Sea level rise has accelerated in the 21st century and is eating up the coastline at an alarming rate. Studies show that about 64 percent of the Texas coast is eroding at an average rate of 6 feet per year, but some areas are losing more than 20 feet annually. As the sea continues to rise, a 1-foot increase in sea level could cause a 200-foot retreat in the shoreline.[1]

In early August of 2023, we visited Chester Island and Matagorda Island to scout, better understand the area's history, and see some of the current conservation efforts in this

ABOVE
Jay and Tim Wilkinson on Chester Island.

remote part of the coast. Peggy and Tim Wilkinson of Audubon Texas, the state chapter of the National Audubon Society, took us on a late afternoon tour of Chester Island, named for Peggy's late father, who had been a warden on the island for 25 years.

As we approached the island from Port O'Connor, Tim mentioned that what we see of Chester Island today is a shadow of its former self. "When my father-in-law began making trips to this island in the mid-80s, it was about 200 acres. Today, we're looking at about 70 acres, and we're doing everything we can to protect what we've got." As we pulled up to shore, terns and gulls lifted off from the beach. Peggy secured the boat while Tim grabbed a ladder from the top of the embankment. The steep, sandy cliff, roughly 10 feet tall, is a reminder of the toll the elements have taken in the past three decades and how little time we have to protect these invaluable islands.

Chester Island is one of Texas' more than 200 rookery islands that serve as nesting habitat for birds. Audubon Texas holds leases on 177 of them off the state's coast, where it manages, restores, and helps maintain critical habitat for nesting colonial waterbirds and shorebirds. The U.S. Army Corps of Engineers, in partnership with the State of Texas, conservation organizations, and communities created these islands with dredged sediment from the GIWW and continue to receive replenishment from ongoing channel maintenance. The

A synthetic barrier provides some protection to an apartment complex on Galveston Island.

islands built with dredge material symbolize some good that has come from the navigable slice taken out of our sensitive salt marsh and shallow bays. In May 2023, the Texas Waterbird Survey recorded more than 22,000 nesting pairs of colonial waterbirds on Chester Island—including more than 2,300 nesting pairs of Brown Pelicans.

Approximately 5,000 Brown Pelicans were present in Texas when scientists began tracking their status in the early 1900s. By 1964, Brown Pelican numbers plummeted and there were only 50 birds reported along the Texas coast. Factors such as the killing of Brown Pelicans by commercial fishermen due to perceived resource competition and the widespread use of pesticides greatly impacted their numbers.

Recognizing the severity of the situation, the U.S. Fish and Wildlife Service listed the Brown Pelican as an endangered species in 1973. At that time, there were merely six nesting pairs reported in Texas. Collaborative efforts among Coastal Bend Bays and Estuaries Program, National Audubon Society, Texas A&M University, Texas General Land Office, Texas Parks and Wildlife Department, and the U.S. Fish and Wildlife Service shored up funding and monitoring for the birds. Audubon Texas' rookery island leasing and management program, which started in 1923, provided the necessary habitat to safeguard pelicans and establish a foundation for their recovery. These efforts led to a gradual resurgence in numbers and stringent restrictions on pesticide usage which caused eggshells to thin and break during incubation.

By 1983, the pelican population in Texas had increased to 75 pairs, swelled to 530 pairs by 1993, and then skyrocketed in 2003 to 3,706 pairs. When the U.S. Fish and Wildlife Service removed Brown Pelicans from the federal threatened and endangered species list in 2009, there were 3,051 nesting pairs. This extraordinary recovery represents a remarkable turnaround for a species that had dwindled from close to 5,000 individuals in the early 1900s to a mere 50 birds in 1964. Today, the population of Brown Pelicans has rebounded exponentially and exceeds 20,000.

Skip Hobbie and Chrissy train their cameras on young pelicans as some wait for their parents to bring food and others make clumsy attempts to take flight. The young pelicans are unphased by our presence, a sign that they have lived their first few months free from

LEFT
One of Chester Island's juvenile Brown Pelicans.

the fear of predators. The Brown Pelican is a conservation success story, and islands like this are critical to their survival.

Not far from Chester Island is Matagorda Island. At nearly 40 miles long, Matagorda Island has served many roles. It was once part of Karankawa territory, later it became a base of operation for the Confederacy and subsequently the U.S. military, and then grazing grounds for a cattle operation. Currently a state Wildlife Management Area and National Refuge, it is now managed jointly by the U.S. Fish and Wildlife Service and Texas Parks and Wildlife Department. The iron lighthouse on the island's northern edge overlooks Pass Cavallo, one of Texas' five natural inlets. It was initially constructed in 1852 and rebuilt in 1872 after storms and damage inflicted during the Civil War.

Pickle Ragusin, who manages the northern half of Matagorda Island for Texas Parks and Wildlife Department, is our guide for the day. He grew up in the small fishing village of Port O'Connor and spent some of his early career crewing boats around all parts of the Gulf of Mexico. Currently, he oversees roughly 60,000 acres of the island, managing hunts and keeping the remaining World War II–era structures in working order. He keeps a collection of plastic dolls and plastic tea cups on a shelf in the shed. Each keepsake has arrived on the island's beach at different times over the past few years, seemingly coming from the same shipment that fell overboard.

RIGHT
(Top) Without Pickle Ragusin, Matagorda Island Wildlife Management Area manager, we could not have hiked or filmed one of the most remote places on the Texas coast.
(Bottom) On the Mid Coast, Matagorda Peninsula and Matagorda Island are home to some of the state's remaining coastal prairie.

We load up in the back of Pickle's Ford pickup and head out to scout the beach before our upcoming walk. We're joined by Felipe Prieto, who manages the island's southern end for the U.S. Fish and Wildlife Service. We cross a massive set of runways that were part of an airfield built by the U.S. Army Air Forces in 1942 to train bomber pilots. It later supported the U.S. Air Force Strategic Air Command, which was responsible for the country's global air reconnaissance and nuclear strike capabilities from 1946 to 1992. My grandfather flew B-17s during World War II and later piloted planes for the Strategic Air Command. During World War II, he flew 52 missions as the captain of the *Wheel N Deal*, part of the 91st Bomb Group that suffered the greatest losses of any heavy bomb group in World War II. As we stroll over the grass-filled cracks, I wonder if he too walked the same asphalt runway.

ABOVE
Walking the north end of Padre Island.

The lighthouse, abandoned runways, and barracks will remind future generations of this island's human history. If the dunes can hold back the rising water, this island will also provide a glimpse of what the land looked like during the time of the Karankawa, Spanish explorers, and missionaries. The tallgrass prairie, freshwater ponds, Bobwhite Quail, and white-tailed deer are relics of a more verdant past. On other barrier islands, the future has arrived.

Padre Island is the world's longest barrier island. Most of the island is permanently conserved as a national seashore and refuge, though it is flanked at each end by resort communities. It's one of the best examples of an intact barrier island on the Texas coast, with broad and slightly sloping beaches, 50-foot-high dunes, open grasslands, expansive algal flats, and shallow marsh. There is even diversity in the flow of water. Currents running in opposite directions along the coast converge here, depositing shells at Little and Big Shell Beaches in a region otherwise devoid of shells.

Development on this island began in 1829 when the Balli family acquired a Spanish land grant. They founded a ranch that operated until 1840 but abandoned the island in 1844 due to the threat of the United States' looming annexation. Subsequently, ranching continued on the

island as the Singer family, the King Ranch, and later the Dunn family utilized it to graze cattle until 1971. The federal government acquired land and designated it as a National Seashore between 1962 and 1969, officially opening Padre Island National Seashore to the public in 1970.

ABOVE
On the north end of Padre Island, developers dredged canals for residential development in the 1980s, but homes were never built.

The north end of Padre Island bears the signs of a new era for the developable parts of Texas' barrier islands. Developers began constructing a new community on the north end of Padre Island after the causeway connecting Corpus Christi to the island was completed in 1967. They built a 13-foot-high seawall, a hotel, condominiums, and thousands of single-family homes—half linked to artificial finger canals connecting to the Laguna Madre or Packery Channel. Today, about 30,000 people live on the north end of Padre Island, and nearly every acre of developable land is covered by a home, a store, or a golf course. Almost every acre. Whitecap NPI broke ground in May 2023, and according to the developer, their plans include 240 acres of land featuring 600 homes, villas, and condos. They will be the island's "first coastal luxury residential and resort destination."

We may be unable to hold back the Gulf, as our barrier islands have for centuries. However, we seem determined to live dangerously close to its rising tide.

CHAPTER 5

OYSTERS

ARCHITECTS OF THE BAYS

Day: 12
Miles walked: 221
Miles remaining: 149

October 12, 2023

We started on the west bank of the Matagorda Ship Channel at a small island created when the U.S. Army Corps of Engineers dredged the channel in the 1960s.

It was overcast, the clouds were low, the sea was really rough, and the crashing waves created a wall of mist on the beach. We followed a narrow path from the channel across a green, grass-covered hill on the beach. It felt like we were walking through the Scottish Highlands or along the coast of Wales.

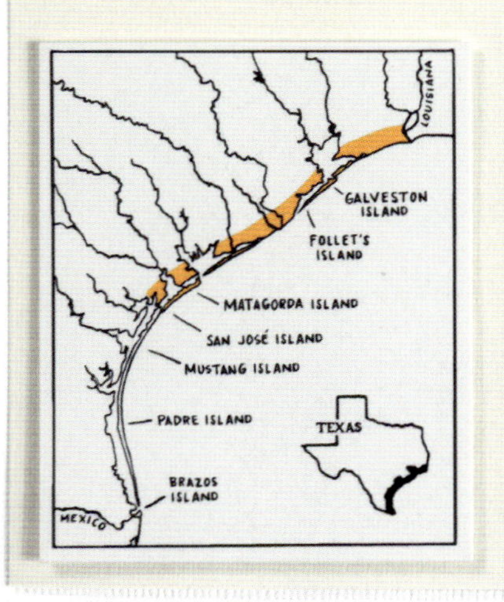

We're feeling more determined than ever right now. It has been raining the past couple of days, and the wind is so strong that our rain ponchos trail behind us like superhero capes. We only walked half a day on Matagorda Peninsula yesterday. Chrissy had a sudden urinary tract infection and has also developed an irritation on the skin of her calves and shins called the "Disney rash." The medical term is exercise-induced vasculitis and is common among visitors to amusement parks. The listed symptoms seemed eerily familiar to our current circumstances — hot weather, sunlight exposure, and sudden, prolonged periods of walking or exercising outdoors.

Pickle Ragusin, our local expert and Texas Parks and Wildlife employee, has been helping us out while we walk and our crew films in the area. Pickle introduced us to Ed and Chantal James a few months ago, and we'd spoken on the phone a few times. Ed and his wife are the only full-time residents of Matagorda Peninsula. Others

have built homes and fishing shacks, but no one else permanently lives out on the peninsula. There are no electric, water, or sewer utilities and access to and from the island is by boat.

Ed and Chantal met us with peanut butter and jelly sandwiches and Dr. Peppers halfway down the 24-mile long peninsula and shadowed us in their 1980s-era four-door Ford pickup. Ed flew Stealth bombers in the U.S. Air Force and qualified for a land grant when he retired. Although Chantal is not fond of the ocean (she only recently stopped wearing latex dishwashing gloves to keep her hands dry while beachcombing), the couple moved to Matagorda Peninsula having never set foot on the place. Today, they live on the edge of an abandoned World War II air base in a house they built by ferrying materials over from the mainland one barge trip at a time.

Not far from where we started, we found a couple of shacks — Matagordaville and the Sand Bar. Hundreds of cabbagehead jellyfish, washed ashore by the high winds and waves, lined the beach. Pickle and our crew

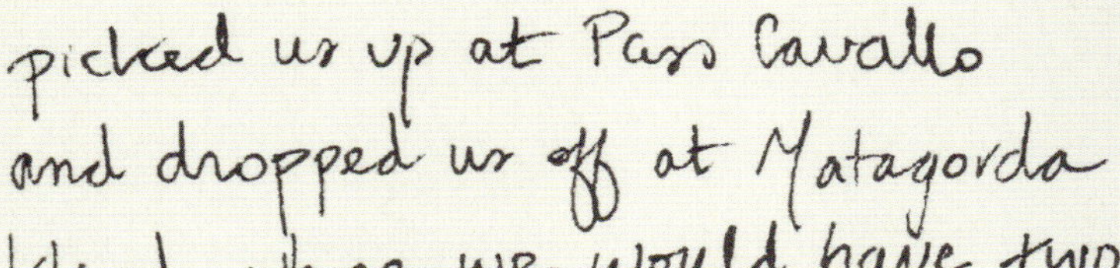

picked us up at Pass Cavallo
and dropped us off at Matagorda
Island, where we would have two solid days of walking.

Once on Matagorda Island, the beach was pretty narrow in places, allowing us to see where the recent high tide had pushed trash up into the dunes, and in other places, the beach was really wide. Just before we got to the lighthouse, we could see where the Gulf had washed over the first line of dunes and cut the secondary dune line in half. We walked to the lighthouse, where we got some beautiful shots with the film crew.

We found three dead giant loggerhead sea turtles on the beach and a lot of trash. Pickle said that volunteers stopped doing trash cleanups in the 1990s once the state park transitioned to a wildlife management area. Without regular visitors to notice, it became harder to convince Texas Parks and Wildlife leadership that cleaning up the beaches was necessary.

Like Matagorda Peninsula, Matagorda Island had an airbase and was part of an active bombing range throughout the first half of the 20th century. By the early 1970s, the island was used more for recreation by the Department of Defense than military exercises. Andy Sansom, former Executive Director of the Nature Conservancy in Texas and Texas Parks and Wildlife, was working at the Department of the Interior at the time and wrote a report exposing the misuse of Matagorda Island by the military. Although it ultimately cost him his job due to pressure from the Secretary of Defense, the island ultimately became a National Wildlife Refuge. It's why

Such a wild place exists today.

We walked 21 miles in 12 and a half hours today. From the west side of Matagorda Island, we took a boat ride back to Port O'Connor. Tomorrow would mark the start of a final 20 miles of hiking on this island, then 20 miles on San Jose Island, and finally, a much-needed day to rest.

As a kid, I remember visiting my grandmother's pink beach house, a few miles south of Port Aransas. Humble Oil ordered the Sears, Roebuck and Co. kit houses and delivered them to Kingsville in the 1930s to accommodate managers of their new oil lease on King Ranch. When the oil company no longer needed the homes, it offered them to a few of my family members. My grandmother accepted one of the homes and had it shipped to Mustang Island, where it was placed behind the second line of dunes. It remains there today.

More than the salty air or the house's eight-bed sleeping porch, I remember most the oyster shell road leading to the house. I couldn't quite understand how those oysters made it so far from the ocean and then neatly lined up to pave the way to the pink house at the top of the dune. I now know that those oyster shells most likely came from the bays around Corpus Christi after a century of overharvesting that began in the late 1800s.

In Texas, oysters were as much a part of early coastal life as freshwater springs were to Indigenous communities farther inland. As early as 3600 B.C., native people harvested shellfish from coastal waters and left shells in mounds, or "middens," near encampments. Some of these middens are evidence of thousands of years of use, stretching for up to a mile and measuring almost 5 feet thick in some areas of the Texas Gulf Coast.

In Corpus Christi and Nueces Bays, the oysters were so thick in some areas that they stretched from shoreline to shoreline. The Karankawas, also known as "water walkers," often used the bays' vast oyster reefs as underwater roadways. Early settlers crossed from Portland to Corpus Christi across the "Reef Road" on horseback, wagon, or buggy. The road was still in use in 1886 when the San Antonio and Aransas Pass Railroad built a trestle bridge alongside it, but finally abandoned as a means of travel when the Nueces Bay Causeway was completed in 1912.[1]

RIGHT
A family shucks oysters in Corpus Christi in 1938. Photo from the Doc McGregor Collection courtesy of the Corpus Christi Museum of Science and History.

As the U.S. and Texas populations increased near the turn of the 20th century, so did the consumption of oysters. Between 1880 and 1910, the American oyster industry boasted production of 160 million pounds of oyster meat per year. Today, that number has dropped by 75 percent. By the early 1900s, other great oyster fisheries had been overharvested or victims of pollution. Despite being home to nearly half the world's oyster population, Manhattan Island was closed in 1922 by the New York City Health Department.[2] Chesapeake

Within sight of Aransas National Wildlife Refuge, winter home of the migrant whooping cranes, a giant dredge—a floating factory—rips away at the bottom of San Antonio Bay, sucking up deposits of oyster shells, washing and sorting them, then spewing a muddy soup back into the shallow ba to smother the life-giving estuaries.

Bay once produced as much as 13 percent of the nation's oysters, but by the 1920s, dredging for oysters had removed three-quarters of the Bay's life-giving reefs.[3] Conversely, Texas' oysters at the turn of the 20th century were in a very different place. In 1900, Corpus Christi was considered to have the best fishing waters on the Texas coast and had four oyster plants and many fish packing houses.[4]

It took another decade for the decline of oysters to begin in the Corpus Christi area. It began with the damming of the Nueces River in 1913. Oysters thrive in brackish water—the combination of fresh water and salt water—in shallow bays and estuaries. Oysters don't inhabit the Laguna Madre, for instance, just a few miles south of Corpus Christi and Nueces Bays due to the lack of significant fresh water from a river or stream between Corpus Christi and Brownsville.

As the damming of rivers continued and the public works projects of the Depression-era '30s resulted in countless reservoirs, it was the fear of drought that sparked the largest decline of oysters. In the decade following the 1950s "drought of record," the state built 2,700 dams to bolster its water supply. Those dams account for about 40 percent of all the dams now in Texas.[5] By 1985, with the completion of Choke Canyon Reservoir, which cut off most of the natural flow to Nueces Bay, the great oyster reefs upon which "water walkers" and settlers had traveled were dead. Today, the Nueces River Estuary has become a reverse estuary where water flows into the river from Nueces Bay, prohibiting the natural exchange of tidal waters.

As the live oyster reefs were starved of fresh water, the need for oyster shells threatened to bury prospects for recovery. The foundation for live oyster reefs is the shell of past generations—layers of shell and sediment dating back to the Pleistocene. That shell became a vital component of the growth of the Texas Gulf Coast during and after World War II. Thanks to cheap energy from large gas deposits and boundless oyster shells, Texas held the position for more than 40 years as the country's top producer and consumer of cement. Shell piles from the middens had long since disappeared, hauled away to shell streets and walkways. Armed with steam power and then massive hydraulic dredges, entrepreneurs learned to plunder oyster reefs for "mud-shell," a mixture of mud and oyster shells hauled up from the bottom of Texas bays.

Some reefs were up to 25 feet thick and as deep as 80 feet under the bay bottom.[6] As they cut deeper into the bays, the dredgers cut through live reefs and disposed of mud in open

LEFT
In 1968, at the height of the battle for oyster shells in Texas bays, *Audubon* published a 16-page article in its magazine and later sued mud shell dredging companies. Courtesy of Dr. Henry H. Hildebrand Papers, Collection 163, Box 39, Special Collections and Archives, Mary and Jeff Bell Library, Texas A&M University–Corpus Christi.

bays, smothering live oysters. Over decades and at times with state oversight, the mud shell dredging industry stripped much of the rough-edged complex of shell and organisms in Texas bays. In 1951, the Texas legislature removed the term "oyster" from the Game, Fish, and Oyster Commission's name. It recognized the declining importance of a once-flourishing industry.

Firms like the Heldenfels Brothers and the Bauer Dredging Company scraped 160,000 tons of shell and bay bottom annually from Nueces, Corpus Christi, and bays farther up the coast. According to a 1967 *Sports Illustrated* article about mud-shell dredging in Texas, oyster shell was used for more than just cement—"The shell is used for paving materials, concrete, chicken and cattle feed, for the manufacturing of plate glass, aluminum, textiles, and dry ice, for fertilizer, soap, magnesium, and many other items—including the Houston Astrodome, which required 500,000 cubic yards of shell in the construction of its stadium and parking lot."[7]

The Audubon Society, which leased and maintained a wildlife sanctuary on the Second Chain of islands in Ayers Bay and part of Matagorda Island, sued the dredging companies in the U.S. District Court for the Southern District of Texas in 1970. The Audubon Society claimed that "as a direct result of the dredging operations, silt, and sedimentary particles are set in motion and that this action is destroying the natural food for the famous Whooping Crane, an almost extinct variety of bird, and the Roseate Spoonbill and other varieties of wild birds known to inhabit these areas. It also alleges that the dredging is destroying the oyster beds and generally upsetting the ecosystem. This, in turn, they allege renders their sanctuary property useless and destroys the value of their leases, as well as that of the Aransas National Wildlife Refuge." Audubon lost the case partly for failing to state damages directly resulting from the dredging operations of the dredging companies.[8]

Mud-shell dredging was finally banned in Galveston Bay in 1969 and ended in Texas bays by the end of the 1970s. By 1980, there were no more oysters in Corpus Christi or Nueces Bay—the result of nearly a century of overharvesting, dredging, and denial of fresh water.

While globally the world has lost close to 90 percent of its historic oyster reefs, the Gulf of Mexico is one of the last places on earth with abundant wild oysters. Even though the

More oyster harvest areas have been closed in recent years

Over the last decade, an increasing number of public oyster harvest areas remained closed at the start of the season because the state did not find enough large oysters in them. This year, only eight are open. The maps show approximate locations of 34 harvest areas in Texas along the gulf coast.

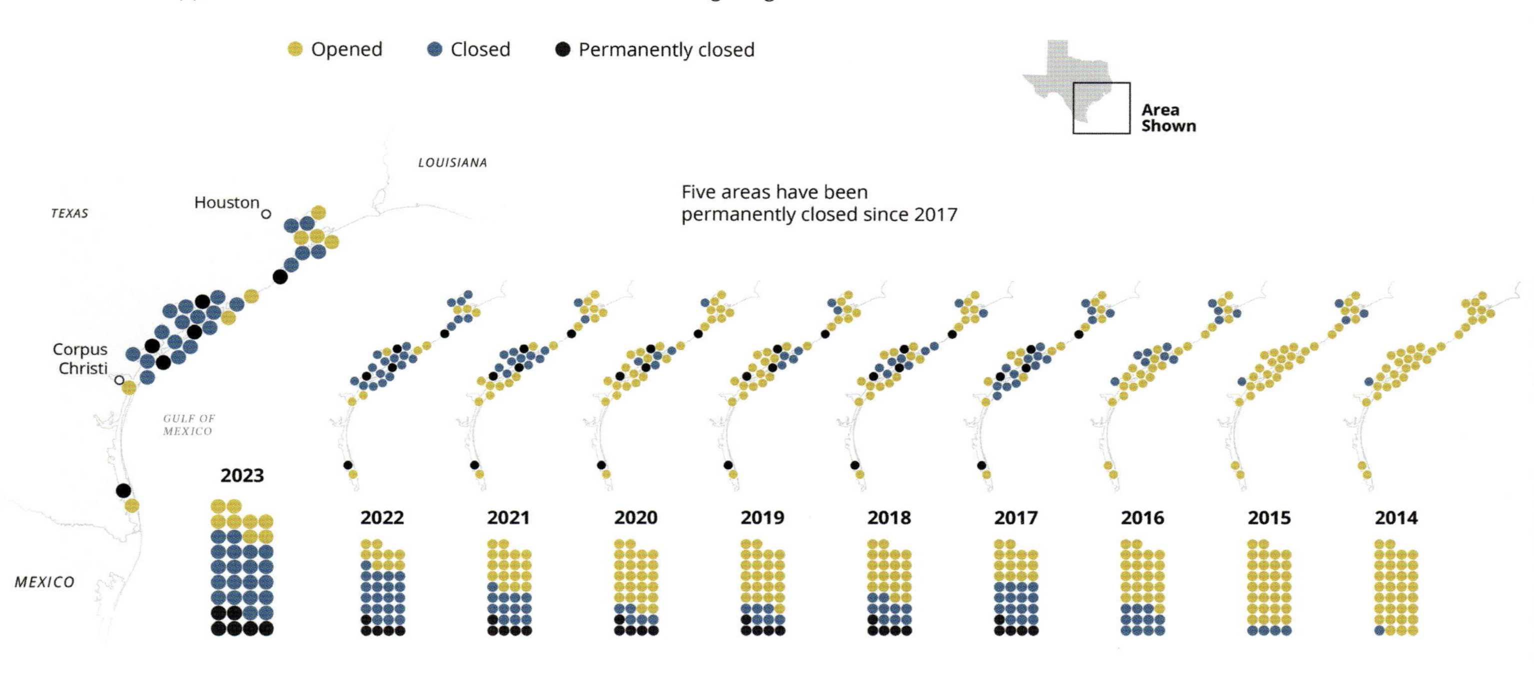

Note: Data includes openings and closings on Nov. 1, which is the beginning of the season each year. Some areas open or close mid-season. Some areas shown as open have minimal to no harvest. Public health closures that are occasionally issued from the Texas Department of State Health Services are not included. **Sources:** Texas Parks and Wildlife Department, Department of State Health Services **Credit:** Yuriko Schumacher

ABOVE
Drought, flood, hurricanes, and over-harvesting have resulted in regulations reducing the number of oysters and bays open to their harvest. Graphic courtesy of Yuriko Schumacher, *The Texas Tribune*.

commercial oyster fishing industry has held on since the 1980s, the past decade has brought renewed focus to the industry's fate and that of remaining wild oysters.

Oyster numbers have been declining in Texas waters for the past decade. Texas Parks and Wildlife Department, the agency responsible for regulating their harvest on public reefs, began closing reefs in 2014 to help them recover. While there are private reefs in Texas, more than 80 percent of harvested oysters come from public reefs. Oyster reefs can sustain some amount of mechanical dredging, but it can take decades to fully restore reef structure to a point that it can support baby oysters and other marine life.

By 2021, only 17 of 34 reefs remained open for more than 450 oyster boats in Texas. When the season opened in November of that year, oyster fishermen from across Texas descended on the remaining open reefs. In the reefs west of Matagorda Island—the Carlos-Mesquite-Ayres

In November of 2021, more than 70 oyster boats descended into a 500-acre area in Carlos Bay. Photo courtesy of John Blaha.

ABOVE
Chuck Naiser and Dr. Jennifer Pollack on Saint Charles Bay, north of Rockport.

complex—a record number of boats scoured the bay bottom for oysters. Texas Parks and Wildlife Department, citing too few legal-sized oysters (3 inches or longer), closed the entire reef complex to harvest by mid-January 2022. Despite early closures that cut the normal harvest season in half, the area accounted for 30.4 percent of coastwide landings in an area that represents only 2.8 percent of total oyster habitat. It was a true tragedy of the commons.

Chuck Naiser, a fishing guide and friend, has seen this battle for a finite resource play out before. He was part of the founding of the Gulf Coast Conservation Association (predecessor to the Coastal Conservation Association), which was formed in the 1970s to prevent the commercial overharvest of redfish and speckled trout by having the state classify them as game fish. I first met Chuck in 2017 after Hurricane Harvey devastated Rockport. He connected me and a group of volunteers from Texas Parks and Wildlife Foundation to residents in need of help in the coastal town. Since that time, Chuck formed an angler-led nonprofit, FlatsWorthy, aimed at protecting habitat in the shallow bays west of San Jose and Matagorda Islands. When the oyster boats showed up en masse in the area in 2021, Chuck and FlatsWorthy took a stand. In a June 2022 *Houston Chronicle* article, Chuck said that the overharvesting of oyster reefs in Carlos, Mesquite, and Ayres bays is "the biggest issue to ever hit this region. The harvest is out of control. The situation is dire. Things have to change."

ABOVE
One of a fleet of more than 70 oyster boats returning to the docks near Rockport, Texas, in November 2021. Photo courtesy of John Blaha.

And things did change. Flatsworthy, the Coastal Conservation Association (CCA), and anglers launched a public campaign to pressure Texas Parks and Wildlife Department to close oyster harvesting, or what Chuck called the equivalent of "strip mining the bays," in the Carlos-Mesquite-Ayres complex. In November of 2022, the Texas Parks and Wildlife Commission voted to permanently close Carlos, Mesquite, and Ayers bays to oyster harvest. The public support was overwhelming, with nearly 80 percent of the public comments in favor of the permanent closures.

Due to environmental impacts, harvest pressures, and the resulting impacts on harvestable oysters, many public oyster harvest areas remained closed at the start of the 2023 season. Only eight of the 34 public oyster harvest areas were open.

We spoke with Dr. Jennifer Pollack, endowed chair for coastal conservation and restoration at the Harte Research Institute for Gulf of Mexico Studies at Texas A&M University–Corpus Christi, about the value of oysters, a movement to restore native habitat, and the reasons to be hopeful about the years ahead. "Over the past two decades, since around 2000, there have been pretty large and consistent declines in oyster populations, not just in Texas, but across the Gulf. We know that oyster reefs just don't seem to be able to catch a break. Hurricanes,

droughts, [oil] spills, and ongoing commercial harvest all impact oyster reefs. When these stressors occur at the same time or in rapid succession, the result can be declining populations of oysters and loss of essential reef habitat."

Oysters are sensitive to fluctuations in water salinity and their environment. Hurricane Ike hit the Upper Texas Coast in 2008, burying nearly 8,000 acres of oyster reefs in tons of sand and sediment from nearby Bolivar Peninsula. The storm wiped out 70 percent of the state's harvest and the livelihood of more than 100 fishing operations. Then Harvey struck in 2017, pouring a historic amount of rain into Galveston Bay. Not only did the reduction in salinity kill oysters, but acidic rainwater from the storm replaced the basic, or slightly alkaline, seawater within the bay, causing the water to be four times more acidic than normal. This extreme acidification lasted for more than three weeks, causing water in the bay to become corrosive to more sensitive larval, juvenile, and adult oyster shells. Scientists had predicted that increasing CO_2 could cause this scale of coastal acidification but did not expect to see it until around the year 2100.[9]

According to Pollack, oyster reefs can provide a buffer against the environmental changes we've experienced and will continue to see. "Oysters are economically and ecologically important to the Gulf of Mexico and the Atlantic Coast of the United States. They are filter feeders, so they open their shells up essentially all day, all night long, and filter water across their gills. By doing that, they're feeding and nourishing themselves and growing, but they're also cleaning and clearing our bay waters. They build these enormous three-dimensionally complex reefs that help break up wave energy and facilitate the growth of other habitats like seagrasses that depend upon clearer waters."

Oysters can also act as a carbon sink, helping capture the very carbon dioxide contributing to climate change. "We're just learning now about the potentially important role that oyster reefs have in capturing and storing carbon. In comparison, we understand this process relatively well for forests, wetlands, and seagrasses. The plants take up CO_2 from the atmosphere via photosynthesis and transfer the carbon to their roots and the sediments around them. Oysters, of course, aren't plants, but they eat enormous amounts of plant material, such as phytoplankton, which have taken up the CO_2 from the atmosphere. Oysters then move this carbon to the sediments and the bay bottom where it gets buried over and trapped from circulation with the atmosphere."

LEFT
Oyster shells help protect Matagorda Island from wave action and rising sea levels.

ABOVE
(Left) An oyster farm in Aransas Bay.
(Right) Skip Hobbie at the Palacios Marine Agriculture Research laboratory filming algae, the food source for oyster larvae.

"The other really important thing that's happening along the Texas coast to preserve oyster reefs is habitat restoration. And this is being done by a number of groups like Harte Research Institute, The Nature Conservancy, and Texas Parks and Wildlife Department," said Pollack. Restoration is occurring in all states across the Gulf of Mexico and beyond. In Texas, conservation organizations are building hundreds of acres of new reefs with substrate from stone, crushed concrete, and even reclaimed oyster shells from local restaurants. "As part of the [restoration] process, this material is transported to areas in the bays where reefs have been degraded or destroyed and put back onto the bay bottom using science to determine the right times and the right places," said Pollack. "It's sort of like *Field of Dreams*. If you build it, they will come. We see oyster larvae attach to those shells or rocks or other materials, and within one year, we have really vibrant, healthy, restored oyster reefs.

"One of the things that oyster reefs are most known for is hosting incredible amounts of biodiversity," Pollack said. "Oyster reefs are essentially the coral reefs of our bay systems. They support diverse numbers of fish, shrimp, crabs, and other organisms you'll find nowhere else. If the oyster reef goes away, those unique assemblages go away with them as well."

In August 2023, the Coastal Conservation Association Texas Executive Board pledged $5 million for oyster reef restoration across the Texas coast. With unanimous approval by all board members present at their August meeting, the CCA Texas board proudly dedicated the funding for future projects in areas protected from commercial harvest.

ABOVE
The Blackjack Point Oyster Company farm in Aransas Bay.

To better understand the state of oysters in Texas and glimpse into their future, our team visited Palacios Marine Agricultural Research (PMAR) in the spring and summer of 2023. Partially constructed inside a trailer to provide mobility during hurricanes, the oyster hatchery produces millions of spat, or oyster larvae, for oyster reef restoration projects and oyster farms in Texas' bays. The team of scientists at PMAR manages the breeding process from spawning to larvae and spat by producing and carefully administering the right amount of live microalgae and water salinity at each life stage. The group expects to produce 15 billion baby oysters annually to benefit Texas farms and coastal waters.

In June 2023, we were on hand to stock the first of 250,000 young oysters on the four-acre Blackjack Point oyster farm in Aransas Bay, owned and managed by AJ and Debbie Minns. The Minns' farm is only the fourth permitted in the state and the first to use Texas-born oysters purchased from the PMAR hatchery up the coast. AJ and Debbie harvested their first bushels of oysters in December 2023 and will coordinate their planting and harvesting schedule to provide hand-raised oysters all year. After more than a century of overharvesting and environmental pressures, oysters are finally receiving the attention and protection they deserve as foundations for the diversity of life on the Texas coast.

CHAPTER 6

REDHEADS AND THE LAGUNA MADRE

WILDLIFE AND WATER IN THE BALANCE

Day: 15
Miles walked: 259
Miles to go: 111

October 13th-15th, 2023

On the morning of the 13th, we got an airboat ride from Felipe Prieto with the Aransas National Wildlife Refuge. He dropped us off at about 8:45 a.m. on the northern end of San Jose Island at Cedar Bayou. We had a busy day ahead of us. We needed to cover 20 miles to get to the 4:00 p.m. ferry from San Jose to Port Aransas.

The day we walked San Jose Island was hot, humid, and without any cloud cover or wind. There were more ghost crabs on the island than on any other part of the coast we've walked. One crab went looking for shade between Chrissy's boots. Today was all business; we just put our heads down and walked fast. We covered 20 miles in six hours.

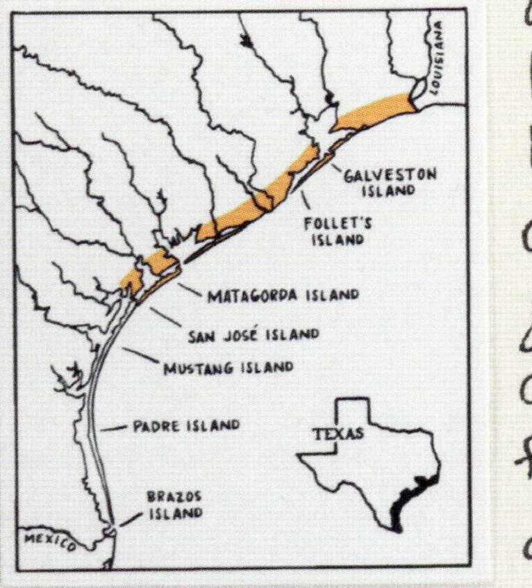

We made the ferry in time and rode across Aransas Pass with a bunch of anglers who had been fishing at the jetty for the day. That night, chef Adam Gonzales cooked paella for us on the beach just south of Port Aransas. He has spent a lot of time fishing along the coast, owns and manages restaurants in Austin and Port Aransas, and runs a fishing lodge in Mexico. Our daughters, some friends from Austin — Michael and Anna Margaret and their two kids — and members of the Harte Research Institute for Gulf of Mexico Studies at nearby Texas A&M University-Corpus Christi joined the gathering on the beach.

We'd been at the same routine for two weeks straight now — wake up at 7 am. in whatever rent home or friend's place we were staying, eat a quick breakfast of cereal and coffee, pack our backpacks with a few pounds of water, snacks, walking poles, rain poncho, sun umbrella, and camera or GoPro, drive with the crew to where we stopped hiking the day before, and walk until sunset or into the night depending on how far we needed to go. After walking nearly 260 miles, eating a chef-prepared meal, and seeing our daughters and friends was amazing.

The next day, we met up with Jace Tunnell, the Director of Community Engagement for Harte Research

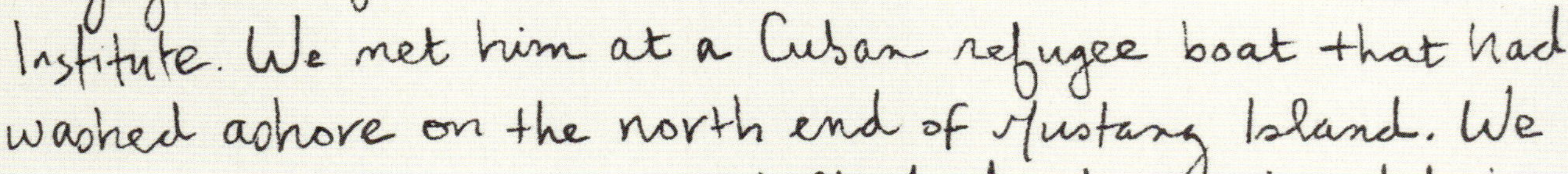

Institute. We met him at a Cuban refugee boat that had washed ashore on the north end of Mustang Island. We talked about marine debris, trash, and creepy dolls. He described how the currents in the Gulf bring a lot of trash to the Texas coastline. More trash, in fact, than any other Gulf state.

On the 15th, we walked from the north end of Mustang Island to Packery Channel. We walked a few miles with Dr. Paula Baker, a volunteer veterinarian at the Amos Rehabilitation Keep, or A.R.K., at the University of Texas Marine Science Institute in Port Aransas. A.R.K. rehabilitates

marine turtles and marine birds in the area around Mustang and San Jose Islands. Our friend, Austin Alvarado, grew up with Paula's son in Austin, Texas and introduced us. We talked about seeing the carcasses of several loggerhead turtles on the beach at Matagorda Island. Dr. Baker said that the cause of their demise may be what's called Debilitated Loggerhead Syndrome. A.R.K. has sent several loggerhead samples to the National Oceanic and Atmospheric Administration, or N.O.A.A., which is studying the illness, but they haven't pinpointed a cause.

Further down the beach, we met a couple and their three children from Dripping Springs. They homeschool their kids and have focused on nature and the environment this year. They have been following our journey on social media and waiting a few days for us to walk by. The kids asked us, "Why on Earth walk the coast when you could drive?" and "What's the coolest thing you've seen?" We didn't have a very good answer for the first question, other than it seemed like a good idea to walk at the time.

What is the coolest thing we've seen? all the people who've helped us out. Not the jaw-dropping response they were hoping for—like a stranded mermaid or buried pirate's treasure—but it was the most honest.

A group of kids from Padre Island joined us as we neared Packery Channel. They formed a cleanup gang about a year ago, ensuring the beach

near their neighborhood remains trash-free. They helped us get our borrowed kayak in the water, and we succeeded in our first self-propelled channel crossing of the trip.

The Upper Laguna Madre from the shoreline of the Norias Division of King Ranch with Padre Island in the background.

Redheads are part of the estimated 80 percent of North American migrant species that travel along the coast of Texas.

THE LAST GREAT HABITAT

SOUTH TEXAS IS CONSIDERED BY SOME WILDLIFE RESEARCHERS TO BE THE LAST GREAT HABITAT BECAUSE WITH MORE THAN 2 MILLION ACRES OF PRIVATE AND PUBLIC LANDHOLDINGS IT IS ONE OF THE LAST REGIONS IN THE STATE THAT CONTAINS EXTENSIVE TRACTS OF CONTIGUOUS AND UNDEVELOPED WILDLIFE HABITAT. IT IS ONE OF THE MOST BIOLOGICALLY DIVERSE REGIONS IN THE WORLD WITH HABITATS RANGING FROM WOODLAND AND WETLAND TO PRAIRIE AND DESERT. THE REGION IS HOME TO MORE PLANT, BUTTERFLY, AND VERTEBRATE SPECIES THAN ANY OTHER PLACE IN THE STATE AND IS A HOTSPOT FOR ENDANGERED SPECIES IN THE UNITED STATES. THE LAST GREAT HABITAT IS ALSO OF HEMISPHERIC IMPORTANCE —MORE THAN 80% OF 332 SPECIES OF LONG-DISTANCE NORTH AMERICAN MIGRATORY BIRDS TRAVEL THOUGH THIS PART OF THE GULF OF MEXICO IN THE SPRING AND FALL.

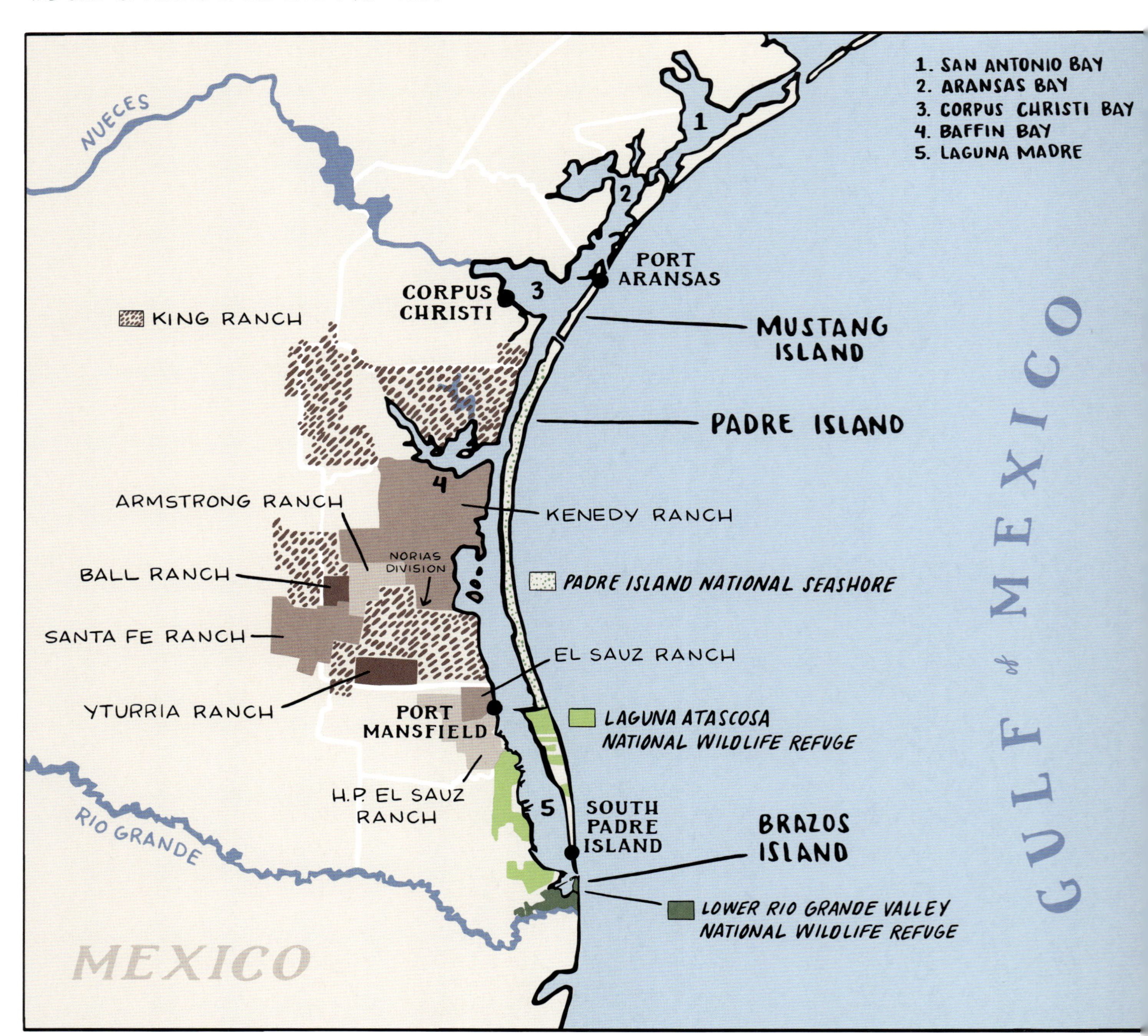

As I look west across a golden sea of grass, the early morning light casts an orange hue on the rolling waves of coastal bluestem. Clumps of rust-colored bushy bluestem leap from the sandy soil, and small, green islands of sacahuiste break up the monochrome landscape. In the distance, 50-foot sand dunes rise above the horizon line on their centuries-old retreat from the sea and slowly swallow windswept live oak trees.

Chrissy and I are on the northeast end of the Norias division of King Ranch in search of freshwater and Redhead ducks. It's been six months since South Texas has had significant rainfall, so only the deepest depressions and ponds fed by solar and wind-powered pumps are holding water. On the way here, we passed a horseshoe-shaped live oak motte where my ancestor, Caesar Kleberg, used to set up a seasonal hunting and fishing camp at the turn of the 20th century.

Caesar was born in Cuero in 1873. He briefly attended St. Edward's University in Austin and then went to Washington, D.C., to work as congressional secretary for his father, Representative Rudolph Kleberg. He returned to Texas in 1900 to work for Henrietta King and his uncle, my namesake and great-great-great-grandfather, Robert Justus Kleberg. Caesar first lived and worked on the Santa Gertrudis division of King Ranch and then moved to Norias, 40 miles south.

Once at Norias, he began a 30-year tenure as a foreman and pioneered wildlife management and conservation practices. The lasting impact of his work and others is apparent as a group of ducks buzz us on their flight path to the same freshwater pond, hidden in this ocean of coastal prairie that we've been searching for to begin *Chasing the Tide*'s first film shoot.

It was Caesar who, with the help of Kineños or "Captain King's men," modified water wells in the pasture so they would overflow into earthen tanks to provide drinking areas for wildlife. In 1912, Caesar implemented the first hunting codes meant to conserve and increase wildlife populations on the ranch. It was a time when statewide game laws were neither well-established nor enforced. I grew up adhering to these same codes, many of which were more strict than state regulations: no shooting game at watering holes, deer season ends when the rut begins, turkey can be taken with a rifle shot to the head or neck,

ABOVE

(Left) Caesar Kleberg hunting at Norias. Courtesy of King Ranch Archives, King Ranch, Inc., Kingsville, Texas. (Right) Caesar with Richard M. Kleberg circa 1915. Courtesy of King Ranch Archives, King Ranch, Inc., Kingsville, Texas.

and no firing at quail when the covey rises. The ranch even protected areas with the most wildlife—like the Laguna Larga, one of Texas' most extensive freshwater wetlands—as sanctuaries where hunting was prohibited.

Caesar was living in precarious times for wildlife. The Texas population was well over 50,000 people in 1836 and had ballooned to more than three million by 1900. Anglo settlers viewed wildlife as a natural resource for both sustenance and profit, significantly affecting the land and wildlife. By 1885, bison had disappeared from the Panhandle Plains. The export trade in wild game came to the nearby waters of the Laguna Madre and Corpus Christi Bay in 1888, with the opening of the San Antonio and Aransas Pass railway, creating even greater disruption.

As Texas laid down track, it connected the state to the national and trans-Atlantic trade in wildfowl—mostly Canvasbacks, plovers, curlews, and Redheads destined for the dinner table and restaurants. As the market for wild game meat expanded in the late 1800s, so did American and European desire for feathers and bird skins to adorn ladies' hats, boas, and dresses. Quill pins from egrets, Roseate Spoonbills, Whooping and Sandhill Cranes, terns,

herons, ibises, pelicans, seagulls, grebes, avocets, skimmers, and other shore and wading birds were also popular at the time.

ABOVE
Scaup and Redheads on Arroyo Colorado, north of Brownsville, Texas. Courtesy of Shannon Tompkins.

Whether by entrepreneurial instinct, morality, foresight, or a combination of all three, Caesar understood the value of wildlife and the pressing need to conserve it. He accurately predicted that someday wildlife would be more productive for the ranch than beef cattle. In the late 1970s, my father, Tio Kleberg, vice president of agribusiness for King Ranch, began implementing the first hunting leases on the ranch. During the 1990s, King Ranch and other South Texas landowners began reporting income from leasing hunting rights, primarily for White-tailed deer and Bobwhite quail, equivalent to or exceeding livestock profits. By 1996, Kleberg County, which contains much of King Ranch, attributed 42 percent of the real estate market value to hunting and outdoor recreation.[1]

Just as the growing railroad network expanded the commercial trade in Texas' game, Caesar expanded his conservation work beyond King Ranch's fence line. He was appointed to the state's Game, Fish, and Oyster Commission in 1917 and then in 1925, alongside his aunt Alice Kleberg, urged Texas governor Miriam "Ma" Ferguson to establish 68 state game preserves totaling 3.2 million acres to help dwindling populations of White-tailed deer, quail, black bear, pronghorn, desert bighorn sheep, and turkey. The preserve system allowed landowners to sell hunting privileges in exchange for actively managing their lands to protect game populations. King Ranch set aside 414,313 acres as a preserve from 1925–1935. By 1928, deer and turkey were abundant enough to be shipped to stock-depleted areas.

As for waterfowl in the 20th century, two key pieces of legislation were critical to staving off their decline due in part to overhunting, drought in the heart of waterfowl breeding grounds, and the draining of millions of acres of marsh nesting sites for farming. The Migratory Bird Treaty was a critical first step in controlling unregulated waterfowl hunting. The treaty was a conservation agreement initially signed in 1916 by Canada and the United States and was the first legal document in the world that made it unlawful to: "pursue, hunt, take, capture, kill, possess, sell, purchase, barter, import, export, or transport any migratory bird, or any part, nest, or egg, or any such bird, unless authorized under permit."

Caesar worked with his cousin, U.S. Representative Richard M. Kleberg, on creating and passing the second bit of legislation to protect waterfowl, the Migratory Bird Hunting and Conservation Stamp Act, also known as the Duck Stamp Act. It required hunters of migratory waterfowl in the U.S. to purchase a stamp, and the resulting revenue provided crucial funds to the federal government to acquire, administer, and maintain wetlands as waterfowl sanctuaries and refuges. The Duck Stamp Act would return a portion of drained land to wetland habitat and preserve unaltered marshlands. Since 1934, more than $1.1 billion has been raised from sales of Federal Duck Stamps helping to conserve upward of six million acres of land within the National Wildlife Refuge System.

Caesar Kleberg died a bachelor on April 14, 1946. Before his death, he drafted his will to include a bequest of $10,000 as well as oil, gas, and mineral rights. The fund was established to aid in the conservation of game and other wildlife in Kenedy and Kleberg Counties. The trustees of the fund were authorized "to expend the income as they deem best . . . in the propagation and conservation of game and other wildlife."[4] He established the first wildlife conservation foundation in Texas, the Caesar Kleberg Foundation for Wildlife Conservation. Over the past 60 years, his foundation, on which I now sit with my brother and father, has given more than $40 million to wildlife research projects and has created endowed

RIGHT
(Top) A waterfowl hunting excursion during the early 1900s on the Corpus Christi pleasure yacht, *Japonica*, displaying hundreds of mostly Northern Pintails and Redheads. Courtesy of Jim Moloney.
(Bottom) Richard M. Kleberg and his quail hunting dog. Courtesy King Ranch Archives, King Ranch, Inc., Kingsville, Texas.

12 PERSONS
12 PERSONS
122 CU.FT.
JAPONICA

ABOVE
Millions of acres of private ranches and public lands surrounding the Laguna Madre are critical to almost the entire wintering Redhead population.

positions at six universities. In 1981, the foundation created the Caesar Kleberg Wildlife Research Institute, whose mission is to provide science-based information for enhancing the conservation and management of wildlife in South Texas and related environments.

The work done by the Caesar Kleberg Wildlife Research Institute's work brings Chrissy and me to this small pond on the Norias coast. A couple of weeks ago, we connected by phone with Dr. Bart Ballard, the Institute's endowed chair in waterfowl research, and we described to him the story we were trying to tell and the imagery we were attempting to capture. He suggested that we focus on the importance of the Laguna Madre—not just to the estimated 80 percent of North American migrant species that travel along the coast of Texas, but to one particular species of duck, the Redhead.

Dr. Ballard has spent much of his career studying migratory birds on the Texas coast. In a three-year study published in 2017, Ballard and a group of scientists used radar technology to monitor migratory bird movements at six locations along the Laguna Madre. They found that the passage rates of migratory birds on the Lower Texas Coast were among the highest recorded for any location in the world.

The Laguna Madre of Texas is critical to almost the entire wintering Redhead duck population. Having spent the spring and summer months in the prairies of the United States and Canada, they migrate here to feed almost exclusively on submersed aquatic

vegetation, especially shoal grass, which has historically thrived in the clear, shallow, and salty waters of this 130-mile coastal stretch. With limited freshwater inflow and some of the highest evaporation rates in the U.S., salinity levels in the lagoon typically ranged from 200 to 300 percent that of seawater.

The hyper-saline nature of the Laguna Madre was permanently altered in 1946 when the Intracoastal Waterway opened up the bays and estuaries to the Gulf. The new, less salty environment provided an opening for less salt-tolerant grasses like manatee grass and turtle grass, which are now rapidly displacing shoal grass. Since 1965, the U.S. Geological Survey estimates that due to the combined effects of increased freshwater inflow and sediment load from dredging, shoal grass has declined by more than 40 percent in the Laguna Madre, and this trend is expected to continue, especially in the upper portions of the estuary.

Redhead populations have reached record highs in recent years due to carefully managed hunting seasons and restored habitat in the Southern Great Plains, stretching from Nebraska to the Texas Panhandle. This increase in numbers may put more significant pressure on the remaining shoal grass beds. Studies conducted in the late 1980s suggest that Redhead populations consumed as much as 75 percent of shoal grass rhizomes, or rootstalks, produced in a given year in parts of the Laguna. Under current population levels, Redheads may exhaust their food supply before returning to their breeding grounds in the northwestern U.S. and southern Canada.

Padre Island has beautiful stretches of beach and thousands of acres of untouched wildlife habitat.

Dr. Ballard's research and his knowledge of Redheads' use of freshwater wetlands, like the one we're scouting for the film, have helped him and other researchers determine that the proximity and the distribution of available freshwater wetlands have an impact on overgrazing of shoal grass beds. To cleanse their bodies of the high salt levels they consume while feeding on shoal grass, Redheads must travel several times daily to inland ponds, where they drink large quantities of fresh water. Ballard and the Caesar Kleberg Wildlife Research Institute are working with conservation groups and private landowners to restore freshwater wetlands and increase the availability of continuous water sources along a greater range of the Laguna Madre coastline.

The human-induced challenges for waterfowl, like the Redhead, on the Lower Texas Coast are no less daunting than at the turn of the 20th century. In this century, thousands of wind turbines have been installed along the Laguna Madre coastline, altering ducks' use of freshwater wetlands. A study by Ballard and others published in 2018 also predicted that sea level rise will inundate 93 of the known 156 coastal freshwater ponds, critical to waterfowl survival, with salt water by 2100.

As Chrissy and I glass the pond with binoculars and count roughly 300 Redheads, something catches my eye. To the north, on the 235,000-acre Kenedy Ranch, a wind turbine blade flashes white as it rotates at nearly 200 miles per hour. While looking at the hundreds of turbines that dot the coastline, something else catches my attention. This time, it's to the east, toward the Laguna and Padre Island. The bleach-white wheelhouse of a barge slowly rolls by on its way from Brownsville north along the Intracoastal Waterway. The economic growth that Caesar and my ancestors hoped for had arrived. Texas is exporting fossil fuels—the same oil and gas that fueled the development of the Caesar Kleberg Foundation for Wildlife Conservation—and now tapping energy from the sun. The land is facing similar pressures from a growing population as it did a hundred years ago but on a much larger scale and a more rapid pace. The future of Texas' wildlife, like the Redhead, depends on how quickly species react and adapt to a changing environment, how well they compete for limited food and water, and the importance Texans place on their survival.

LEFT

Freshwater ponds near the coast attract all forms of wildlife, including coyotes, Sandhill Cranes, and Northern Harriers.

Dr. Bart Ballard on North Padre Island.

A freshwater pond on the Norias Division of King Ranch.

Passage rates of migratory birds on the Lower Texas Coast are among the highest recorded for any location in the world.

CHAPTER 7

KEMP'S RIDLEY

THE WORLD'S MOST ENDANGERED SEA TURTLE

Day: 18
Miles walked: 318
Miles remaining: 52

October 18, 2023

We walked another 18 miles on Padre Island National Seashore yesterday. It is the best example off an intact barrier island we've seen — sloping beaches and coppice dunes acting as foothills between the beach and larger dunes. The sand dunes off our right shoulder were almost 20 feet tall and were up to 100 feet tall in the second line of dunes beyond view.

We figured out we could make it to the Mansfield Cut at the southern tip of the Seashore. It's one of the most significant developments of the trip. Park staff told us when we crossed into the National Seashore that we couldn't make it off the island's southern tip due to the recent high tide. The park ranger with whom we spoke said that no vehicles or people had

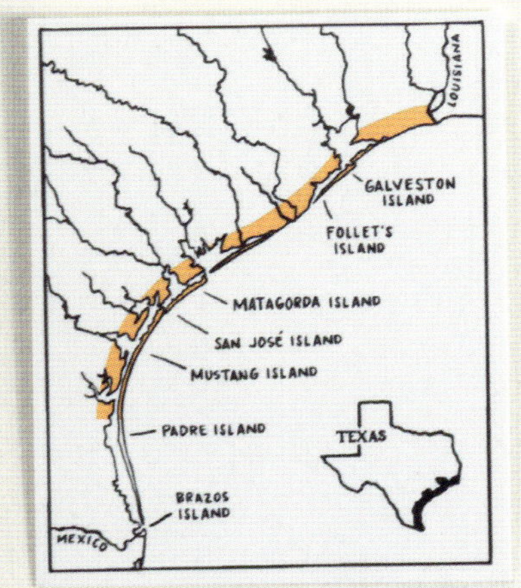

gone that far south in days out of fear of being stranded between the low and high tides.

Had we not overcome so many obstacles to get this far — construction at McFaddin Beach, thunderstorms throughout the first week, finding a boat ride across the Brazos River, and covering 300 miles in 18 days — Chrissy and I would have been worried about this news. Short of a hurricane making landfall, we were determined to make it to the Rio Grande.

As has become the trend, Ellis volunteered to drive his truck to the end of the island to ensure we could continue our journey. He set out yesterday morning and caught up to Chrissy and me on the beach after a five-hour, 120-mile round trip to Mansfield's Cut. He reported that there were trucks and anglers scattered all the way down to the Cut, and the tide was subsiding, which meant we'd be able to walk and get vehicular support.

We finally got a hold of Gene Gore last night. He said that

he could support us once we cross Mansfield Cut to South Padre Island. On our final day, he will arrange a boat to ferry us across the Brazos Santiago Pass and make the final walk to Boca Chica.

We had our first television interview with one of the local stations out of Corpus Christi and then spent most of the morning walking and talking with the film crew as they sat on the back of Ellis's truck. We recounted the last 18 days in surprising detail, island by island, and pass by pass. We were reminded of some of the hardships, the weather delays, the heat and the wind, and body aches and ailments. For the most part, though, we'd already moved on from the challenges and had our sights on finishing.

What sticks with us is a sense of wonder and appreciation for everyone we've met who helped us get to this point. Chrissy and I have a new respect for eachother and feel fortunate to see Texas and Texans in a new light. We keep thinking about this trip and all the people who believe in us and our team.

We have another three or four hours to go today, and the weather is amazing with only a little bit of a headwind, and the water is emerald green.

Chrissy is up in the dune area now with her head down, scouring the sand for treasure. She's at least a hundred yards from the water. The tide has pushed trash and debris up there and is where she's spent most of her day. She can't stay near the crashing waves and hard-packed beach for too long for fear of missing an interesting light bulb, doll head, or glass bottle from another part of the world. Just in the past hour she's found two 500 peso bills and a dozen swim goggles.

We'll be happy to see our girls soon. It will be saddening to leave this journey which has such a simple and meaningful purpose, but we are already thinking about the next adventure.

When we're not listening to music — Robert Ellis' "How I Love You," Bon Iver's "Hazelton," and rap and country from the '90s have been on repeat of late — deciding whether or not a found shell is worth putting in one of our backpacks, trying to identify birds before their hurried runs turn to effortless flight, we're talking about what the past few weeks have afforded us. It's a single-minded, stripped down version of ourselves and our marriage.

It's as if when we stepped off that airboat at Sabine Pass with the intent of walking to the Rio Grande; we entered a time machine before real jobs, diapers, a home, teenage drama, politics, a pandemic, and shared calendars. Suddenly, we were looking at each other again, really looking at one another, and noticing the little things without the distortion of competing interests, compromise, or ambition.

We realized we'd been on a shared mission, a different kind of journey, for the past 20 years. We just lost sight

of who was on that trek with us — walking every step, carrying part of the load, silently saying, "You got this." It had become clear that over the past 18 days, we had begun to walk in lockstep, sometimes veering into the softer sand in search of treasure or walking in silence, but we were in this together, for better or worse.

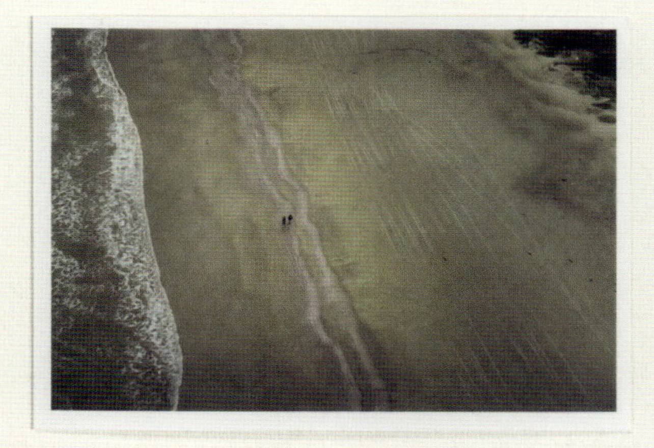

At home in Austin in mid-January 2024, I walked into our bedroom and nearly tripped over the mess. Lenses, open backpacks, cameras, a tripod, stacks of T-shirts and pants, and a pile of socks littered the floor. If this were any other relationship, my heart would have dropped, and panic would have set in. Had I ignored the subtle and not-so-subtle signs? Is this it?

She was leaving, but not for someone else. Well, not another human, at least. A cold snap hit Texas on January 15th, and below-freezing temperatures persisted for a week. In the shallow waters of the Lower Laguna Madre, nearly 1,000 Atlantic green sea turtles were cold-stunned, unable to move in the frigid waters. They were floating on the surface, washed ashore, and rescued by Sea Turtle, Inc. volunteers and staff, a nonprofit sea turtle rescue and rehabilitation group on South Padre Island. Chrissy had already called Wendy Knight, Sea Turtle, Inc. CEO, to tell her she was headed down to interview her and film the rescue effort. "I'll be back," she said as she zipped the last of her bags and headed out the door. *Well, that's comforting*, I thought. *She at least plans to come home.*

We'd met Wendy and her staff in June 2023. We wanted to focus a part of our film project on Kemp's ridley sea turtles, and Sea Turtle, Inc. was a crucial part of their recovery story. The organization's unlikely founder, Ila Loetscher—the first Iowa woman to get her pilot's license—began taking Kemp's ridley eggs that friends had gathered from their nesting grounds in Mexico and burying them in the sand on South Padre Island's beaches in 1963. Loetscher and a group of friends were partly responding to video footage released at a scientific conference in the early 1960s by Dr. Henry Hildebrand of Corpus Christi.

The footage documents a 16-mile stretch of beach at Rancho Nuevo, Tamaulipas, Mexico, in 1947, captured by Andreas Herrera, a young Mexican rancher, engineer, and private pilot. Scientists were amazed when Dr. Hildebrand presented it at the 1961 summer meeting of the American Society of Ichthyologists (a branch of zoology dedicated to the study of fish). It proved what biologists had speculated for years, that even though a single nesting Kemp's ridley had been documented in 1948, it had to be linked to a larger nesting population.

The sheer number of sea turtles in the film was a shock—an estimated 40,000 females were laying eggs on that stretch of beach. Herrera witnessed an *arribada*, a Spanish word referring to the synchronized nesting unique to Kemp's and Olive ridley sea turtles. According to

SEA TURTLES OF THE WORLD

accounts, so many turtles came out of the water to lay their eggs that day that Herrera was stranded for 24 hours before the beach was clear enough to take off in his plane.[1]

Kemp's ridleys are the world's most endangered sea turtle species, named after Richard M. Kemp, a fisherman from Key West, Florida, who first submitted the species for identification in 1906. They are one of only five sea turtle species in the Gulf of Mexico and one of only seven worldwide. It is the smallest of all sea turtles and primarily feeds on crabs but also shrimp, snails, clams, jellyfish, sea stars, fish, and occasionally marine plants. While their primary geographic range is the Gulf of Mexico, they also extend up the eastern coast of the U.S. to New England and Nova Scotia.

The Kemp's ridley is the only sea turtle that nests primarily in the daytime. It is also the fastest nester, emerging from the water, digging a nest, laying up to 130 eggs, covering them, and returning to the ocean all in 45 minutes. Other sea turtle species take an hour and a half to four hours.

When Dr. Hildebrand discovered Herrera's film in the early 1960s, the Kemp's ridley population was declining due to the overharvesting of eggs on nesting beaches and the loss of juveniles and adults due to commercial fishing. In addition to discovering the

ABOVE
Kemp's ridley sea turtle hatchlings on South Padre Island.

arribada, the footage revealed another shock—it depicted individuals collecting turtle eggs immediately after they were laid, loading them by the millions onto trucks for consumption. Some of the nesting females were also captured. According to scientists, approximately 90 percent of the turtle nests were pillaged on the very day they were laid.[2]

In 1966, the Mexican government enacted laws to safeguard the beach at Rancho Nuevo, deploying guards to prevent harvesting eggs and turtles. Despite these protective measures, the annual count of Kemp's ridley nests consistently declined. The United States placed Kemp's on the Endangered Species list in 1970 to enhance protection for the turtles.

In 1978, the United States collaborated with Mexico in an international initiative to rescue the Kemp's ridley species from extinction and bolster its population. Comprehensive programs involving multiple agencies were established in both countries, including establishing a secondary nesting colony at Padre Island National Seashore.

Between 1978 and 1988, more than 20,000 eggs were collected, packed in sand from Padre Island, and transported from Rancho Nuevo to Padre Island National Seashore. After incubation in "corrals," protected locations on the beach, the hatchlings were released onto the sand to imprint on that specific area. Subsequently, the hatchlings were captured and transferred to a specialized facility at the National Oceanic and Atmospheric Administration's

National Marine Fisheries Laboratory in Galveston. There, they were nurtured for approximately one year before being released in various locations, including Mustang and the northern part of Padre Island. This program gave the turtles time to grow, enhancing their ability to evade numerous predators and thereby increasing their chances of survival.

Despite all these efforts, the turtle population continued to dwindle, reaching a low in 1985 with only 702 nests worldwide. In 1992, the National Oceanic and Atmospheric Administration (NOAA) established regulations mandating turtle excluder devices in shrimp trawl fisheries to mitigate sea turtle bycatch. The number of nests and eggs started to rise in the 1990s, and by the mid-2000s, the numbers showed promising improvement.

By 2009, the Texas coast reported nearly 200 nests, while Rancho Nuevo was home to an estimated 20,000. In 2013, Texas designated the Kemp's ridley the state sea turtle. In recent years, Kemp's have primarily returned to Padre Island, Padre National Seashore, and South Padre Island but have been documented nesting as far up the coast as Bolivar Peninsula. In 2023, Padre Island National Seashore reported 144 nests, and South Padre Island, where Sea Turtle, Inc. operates, reported 73 nests.

Because Kemp's nest during the day, the females and their eggs are vulnerable to vehicular traffic on the beach and predators, like feral pigs, coyotes, raccoons, birds, and crabs. If not for the efforts of organizations like Sea Turtle, Inc., Padre Island National Seashore, and others, the turtles nesting in Texas wouldn't stand much of a chance of survival.

Annually between April 1 and August 15, Sea Turtle, Inc. interns and volunteers conduct daily patrols in the 60 miles of beach on South Padre Island and Boca Chica, looking for sea turtle nesting activity. Once a nesting female is found, staff tag the turtle, take a biopsy sample, and collect measurements for collaborative research studies. When the nesting female is back in the water, they excavate her eggs and relocate them to a "corral." After 45 to 55 days, hatchlings emerge from the nest cavities, and Sea Turtle, Inc. releases them to the Gulf of Mexico. During every step of the process, minutes count, meaning that the Sea Turtle, Inc. team doesn't get much sleep during nesting season.

During our film crew's visit to South Padre Island in June 2023, we were on hand for a Kemp's ridley hatchling release. We met Dr. Amy Bonka with Sea Turtle, Inc. before sunrise near the beachside turtle egg incubation "corral." From there, we drove north to a release

SEA TURTLE INC.
243-4361

(Left) Dr. Amy Bonka carefully removes newly-laid Kemp's ridley eggs from a nest to transfer them to a secure incubation site.

(Right) Dr. Amy Bonka of Sea Turtle, Inc. measures a newly hatched turtle on South Padre Island.

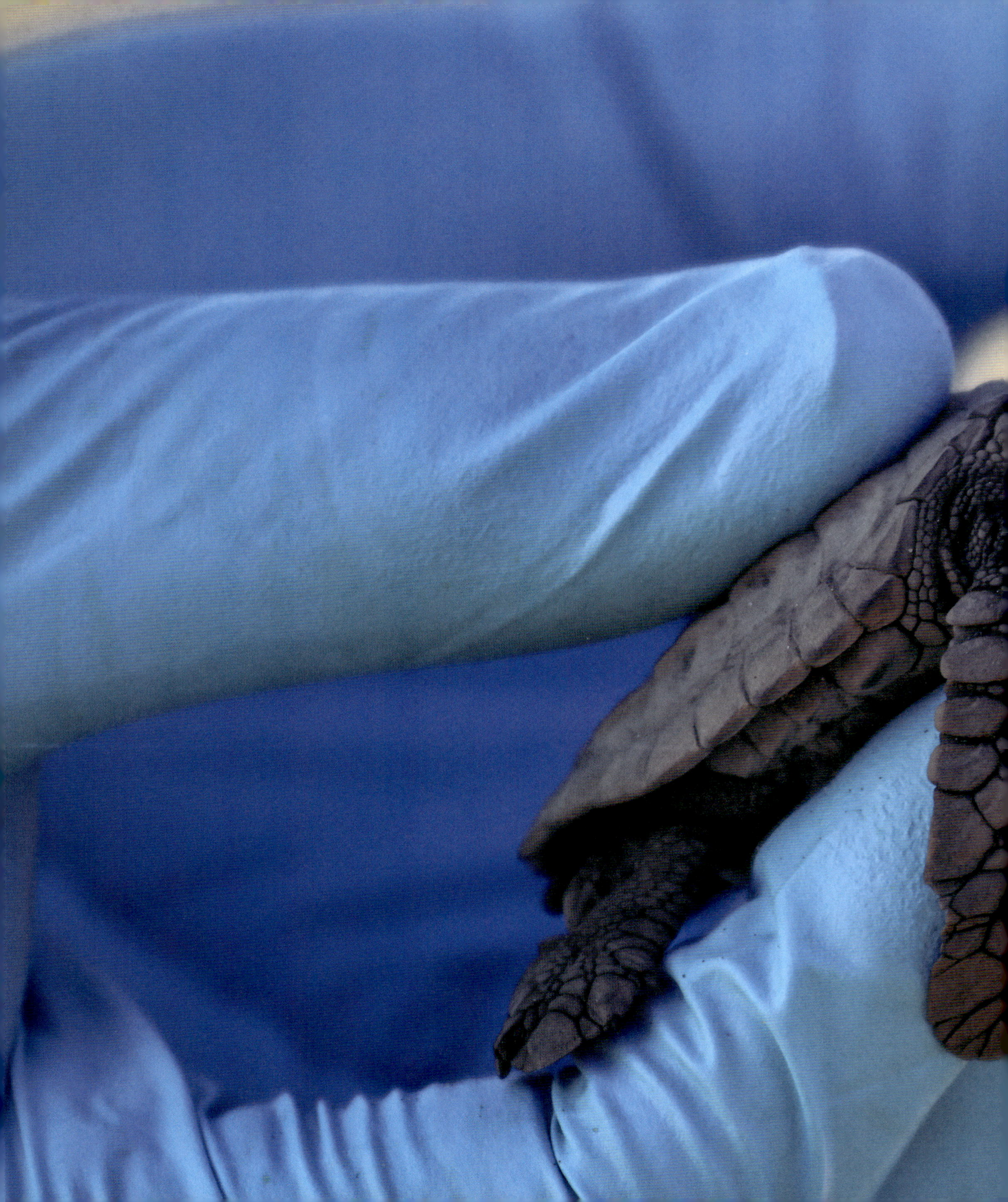

A pair of sea turtle hatchlings moments before being released into the Gulf of Mexico.

ABOVE
After being collected on South Padre Island, these Kemp's ridley sea turtle eggs incubate in Sea Turtle, Inc.'s "corral."

site on the beach, several miles from beachside hotels and condominiums, where Dr. Bonka took several tiny sea turtles—small enough to fit in her palms—and placed them on the wet sand facing the oncoming waves.

"They use gravity as cues when they're in the nest," she explained, "and work against gravity to climb out of the sand. Once they get out [of the nest], their senses switch from reacting to gravitational cues to depending on light cues. They're going towards bright, open horizons and away from dark shadows and silhouettes. Once they get near the surf, they'll typically swim directly into the oncoming waves and keep swimming."

As we watched the hatchlings use their flippers to cover the short distance to the tide line, Dr. Bonka described the journey about to begin. "They're going to fight all those waves and then go out into what we call convergent zones, which are areas where different currents converge on each other. They'll search for large, floating mats of *Sargassum* [algae], which provide them a place to hide and feed." She explained that they can live up to six years around the protection of these islands of brown seaweed. Later they begin to move inshore and feed in near-shore waters.

The Kemp's ridley sea turtles that hatch on South Padre will feed off the coasts of Florida and the Yucatan and then find their way back to this very beach to nest. "It's why we put them down on the sand and let them crawl in the water instead of putting them directly in the water," said Dr. Bonka. "Crawling down the sand is an important part of the imprinting process. It enables them to know what beach they came from so they can return here and lay their eggs in about 12 years."

ABOVE
Sea Turtle, Inc. hosts a public release on South Padre Island.

When Chrissy returned to South Padre in January 2024, Dr. Bonka and Wendy Knight of Sea Turtle, Inc. were working with an army of volunteers to save a different species of turtle, Atlantic green sea turtles. The turtles had survived last summer's heat and were now battling freezing temperatures.

Chrissy interviewed Wendy at Sea Turtle, Inc.'s rehabilitation and visitors center, which had turned into a warming center for hundreds of turtles. They had been placed in blue, plastic kiddie pools. Mrs. Knight explained, "Sea turtles are cold-blooded animals, and they use the water temperature to regulate their body temperature. It's one of the reasons why sea turtles love the waters around South Padre Island because we have warm weather pretty much year-round," she explained. "When we have unusually cold weather, it creates quite a challenge for cold-blooded animals like sea turtles. Their core body temperature drops, and even though they're awake and alert, they can't move their flippers to swim or raise their heads to breathe," she continued. "They float to the surface of the water, and if they aren't rescued or pushed onto dry land by the wind, they will drown, unable to raise their head to take a breath."

The Sea Turtle, Inc. team, along with Texas Parks and Wildlife Department members, Texas Game Wardens, the Coast Guard, as well as community members, rescued and released 950 Atlantic green sea turtles. So many sea turtles had succumbed to the frigid waters after surviving one of the hottest summers on record. As hundreds of sea turtles lay on the floor before her, Chrissy wondered what toll these rapid changes in water temperature and longer and hotter summers had on these animals. This freeze marked the second-largest cold-stun event recorded in Sea Turtle, Inc.'s 46-year history.

ABOVE
In January 2024, Sea Turtle, Inc. headquarters and gift shop became a makeshift rescue and recovery center.

The clues to the long-term impacts of climate change lie beneath the shells of the 950 turtles rescued from the shallow waters of the Laguna Madre that week. Wendy Knight explained, "You actually can't tell the gender of a sea turtle until they've reached adulthood. You can tell [gender] because male sea turtles have long tails extending past their shell or carapace, and females' tales remain much shorter." Sea Turtle, Inc. staff estimated that 20 percent of the nearly 1,000 Atlantic green sea turtles retrieved from the water during this cold stun event were males. Knight continued, "The hotter the sand is when they're incubating, the more females produced. Women are hot, and men are cool." As Texas and its beaches get hotter, we could see fewer male sea turtles available to breed with an increasing number of female sea turtles.

Kemp's ridley sea turtles face astounding odds of survival—one in 800 hatchlings will make it to adulthood. After being released into the water, they must escape hungry fish and diving seagulls and find refuge in floating Sargassum islands far from shore. They will circumnavigate the Gulf of Mexico for years, searching for blue crabs, fish, jellyfish, and sea urchins in shallow waters before finally returning to their birthplace to live and reproduce. One percent of the Kemp's ridley population calls Texas home. For those lucky few, there's an army of people working day and night to give them a fighting chance of survival.

Two green sea turtles recover indoors after being rescued from freezing temperatures.

A Sea Turtle, Inc. staff member releases a rehabilitated Atlantic green sea turtle.

CHAPTER 8

NORTHERN APLOMADO FALCONS

RETURNING TO THE COASTAL PRAIRIE

Day: 19
Miles walked: 338
Miles remaining: 32

October 19, 2023

The end of the 18th was brutal. We had a 15-mile-an-hour headwind and full sun. It made for a top-three tough day because it never let up. Even though the conditions were tough, Chrissy still spent all of her time in the deeper sand near the dunes beachcombing. She found more pesos and another kilo of cocaine. We came across our first package, wrapped in black plastic, a week ago.

We promptly notified Customs and Border Protection and returned to Padre that night, stopping at a gas station for snacks and Whataburger for dinner. At the gas station checkout counter, we set down two Coke ICEEs, two Snickers, and two packs of powdered donuts. After scanning everything, the female attendant looked up at us and said sarcastically, "sweet tooth, huh?"

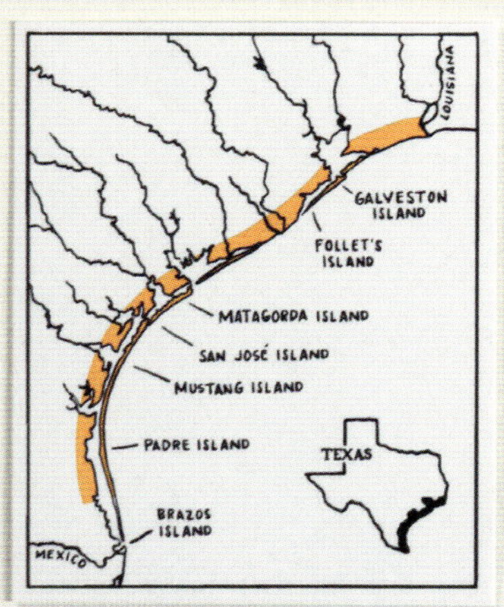

We saw border patrol agents again today.

One stopped us this morning while we were on our way south to mile marker 40. We told him about one of the kilos we found, and he followed us to where we marked it with a GPS pin. As he returned to his vehicle, he asked if we were the couple walking the entire coastline. "Oh my God, my wife is following you on Facebook. Can I get a picture with you?" After taking a picture, Chrissy gave him a Chasing the Tide sticker to give to his wife. We saw another border patrol agent right as we came across another wrapped block of drugs. We told him about it, and he said he'd be there a while doing paperwork.

Later that day, we met a couple, Jimmy and Tracie Lynn Rutledge from Fredericksburg, where Jimmy owns the Family Hair Cuts Barbershop. They had their two dogs, Bear and Molly, in the truck with them. Jimmy and Tracie Lynn held our hands and prayed for us before driving off.

On the 19th, we passed Big Shell Beach, where converging

currents deposit shells. The southern end of Padre Island National Seashore differs from the northern section. The sand changed – it was delicate and dark brown. The water was clear, and we saw fish feeding in the breaking waves. The sand dunes were smaller, and we could occasionally see the Laguna Madre to the west.

Chrissy ran into a guy who had attended the same high school as her in San Antonio. While they were reminiscing about old friends and how that part of the city has grown, I thought how wild it was that they'd run into each other on this island.

It was another long, hot day – nine hours on foot. By the time we got to the jetties at Mansfield Cut, we were spent. The funny thing about jetties and passes along the coast is that you can see them for miles. It takes forever to reach them and yesterday was no exception.

We arrived at the Cut at 4:30 p.m., and that's precisely when our new friend and fly fishing guide, Ben Paschal from Port Mansfield picked us up in his poling skiff. He beached just on the Western edge of the jetty, handed us a couple of Lone Stars, and we were on our way into town.

We were surprised to see oyster reefs along the edge of the ship channel despite the high salinity levels. Ben said that because of the flow exchange between the Laguna Madre and the Gulf, salinity levels dropped enough to allow oysters to grow.

Reporter Christian Von Preysing and his colleague Cynthia were waiting for us at the Port Mansfield Marina. They were there to interview us for the local news. Afterward, they gave us a ride to the Sunset House Motel and RV Park, where management left the key in the door to our room for us.

We had dinner at the Windjammer restaurant and ordered two Cokes, mozzarella sticks, an all-you-can-eat salad bar, two fried shrimp platters, and pecan pie for dessert.

We've burned about 5,000 calories daily for nearly three weeks, and the Windjammer hit the spot.

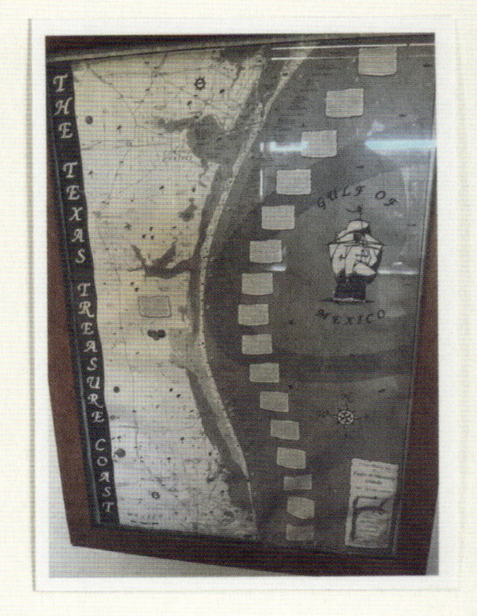

One of the walls displayed a map of all the shipwrecks on Padre Island from the 1800s through the 1980s. After dinner, we grabbed supplies at the local bait shop and promptly fell asleep in our bed at the Sunset House Motel and RV Park.

An adult Aplomado watching from a distance.

It's been nearly 20 years since Chrissy's held an Aplomado Falcon or seen any former colleagues from The Peregrine Fund. We were newly married and living in El Paso when she took a summer job as a "hack site" attendant. Groups like The Peregrine Fund use hack sites to reintroduce raptors into a new environment. The "hack," or release, boxes serve as surrogate nests for chicks as they grow.

Chrissy, passionate about her work with The Peregrine Fund, spent one summer living in an old concrete ranch house with no air-conditioning and an outhouse with a resident barn owl. Another summer, she and her colleagues lived in a small house off the railroad tracks in Valentine, named for the day the crew of the Southern Pacific Railroad reached the site in 1882. When I would visit, we'd drive to Marfa to hang out in the air-conditioning, play Scrabble, and drink coffee at the Marfa Book Company. Marfa has attracted many celebrities and artists since the movie *Giant* was filmed there in 1956, and minimalist artist Donald Judd made it home for his family and work in 1979.

When she took that position in 2005, The Peregrine Fund saw early success in restoring the Northern Aplomado Falcon to its historic range in South Texas. They decided to expand their work to private ranches in West Texas. In 2002, The Peregrine Fund raised 36 Aplomado chicks in captivity at their headquarters in Boise, Idaho, then flew the chicks 1,200 miles by plane to the airport in Van Horn, Texas. The young falcons were then placed at hack sites on the open prairie of several private ranches, fed captive-raised coturnix quail, and monitored until they left the site and began to support themselves. Chrissy and the other hack site attendants' job was to keep those young falcons alive until they were old enough to fledge.

She worked several hot summers helping The Peregrine Fund and private landowners restore Aplomado Falcons to the Chihuahuan Desert in West Texas and southern New Mexico. From 2002 to 2012, 686 birds were released in the Marfa area and 337 birds in southern New Mexico.[1] Despite their efforts, The Peregrine Fund team was unsuccessful in establishing a sustainable wild population in either region due to persistent drought, reduced prey populations, and high mortality rates of released falcons from predation by raptors like the Great Horned Owl. It was another setback for a raptor on the brink of extinction in the United States.

LEFT
An adult Aplomado Falcon in South Texas.

Like Aplomados, Peregrine Falcon numbers declined drastically in the 1950s and 1960s due to the widespread use of DDT pesticide. By 1970, the same year The Peregrine Fund was founded, the raptor was judged extinct in the eastern United States, and fewer than 40 pairs were estimated in the West. That same year, the U.S. Fish and Wildlife Services placed the American and Arctic Peregrine on the endangered species list. Following the U.S. ban on DDT in 1972, The Peregrine Fund perfected breeding Peregrines in captivity and releasing them into the wild. In 1999, after decades of successful captive breeding, Peregrines reproducing successfully in the wild throughout their range, and increasing migration success, the U.S. Fish and Wildlife Service removed the Peregrine Falcon from the endangered species list.

On the second-to-last day of our walk of the Texas coast, Chrissy and I ran into Sam Voss, a veteran survey volunteer, and Gregg Doney, project leader with Earthspan. They were surveying for migrant Peregrine Falcons, an annual survey now in its 47th year, at Padre Island. They have also been studying Peregrine Falcon migrants at Assateague Island along the Mid-Atlantic coast since 1970. Both Padre Island and Assateague Island are major focal points of the autumn and spring tundra peregrine migration, resulting in the collection of information from Peregrines that covers broad geographic areas from their Arctic breeding/natal areas to their winter ranges that span much of the Americas.

These efforts build on the collective migration stopover studies of falconers and researchers at each site, stemming back to the 1930s and 1940s. In partnership with The Peregrine Fund, this long-term study analyzes the health, distribution, ecology, and population dynamics of Arctic Peregrine Falcons during spring and fall migrations. This collection of decades of research represents the bulk of Tundra Peregrine Falcons banded within the continental United States since the establishment of the Bird Banding Laboratory by the Department of the Interior and constitutes the longest continuous monitoring study of this falcon in the Americas. Long-term studies such as this one are essential to monitoring the stability of wildlife populations, particularly considering rapid changes that may occur due to contaminants, infectious diseases, habitat loss, climate change, and other factors.

As part of this work, Sam, Gregg, and other researchers collect and archive tissues from migrants for assessments of contaminants, like DDT and pathogen exposure of conservation

ARCTIC PEREGRINE FALCON

BREEDING & MIGRATION ROUTES

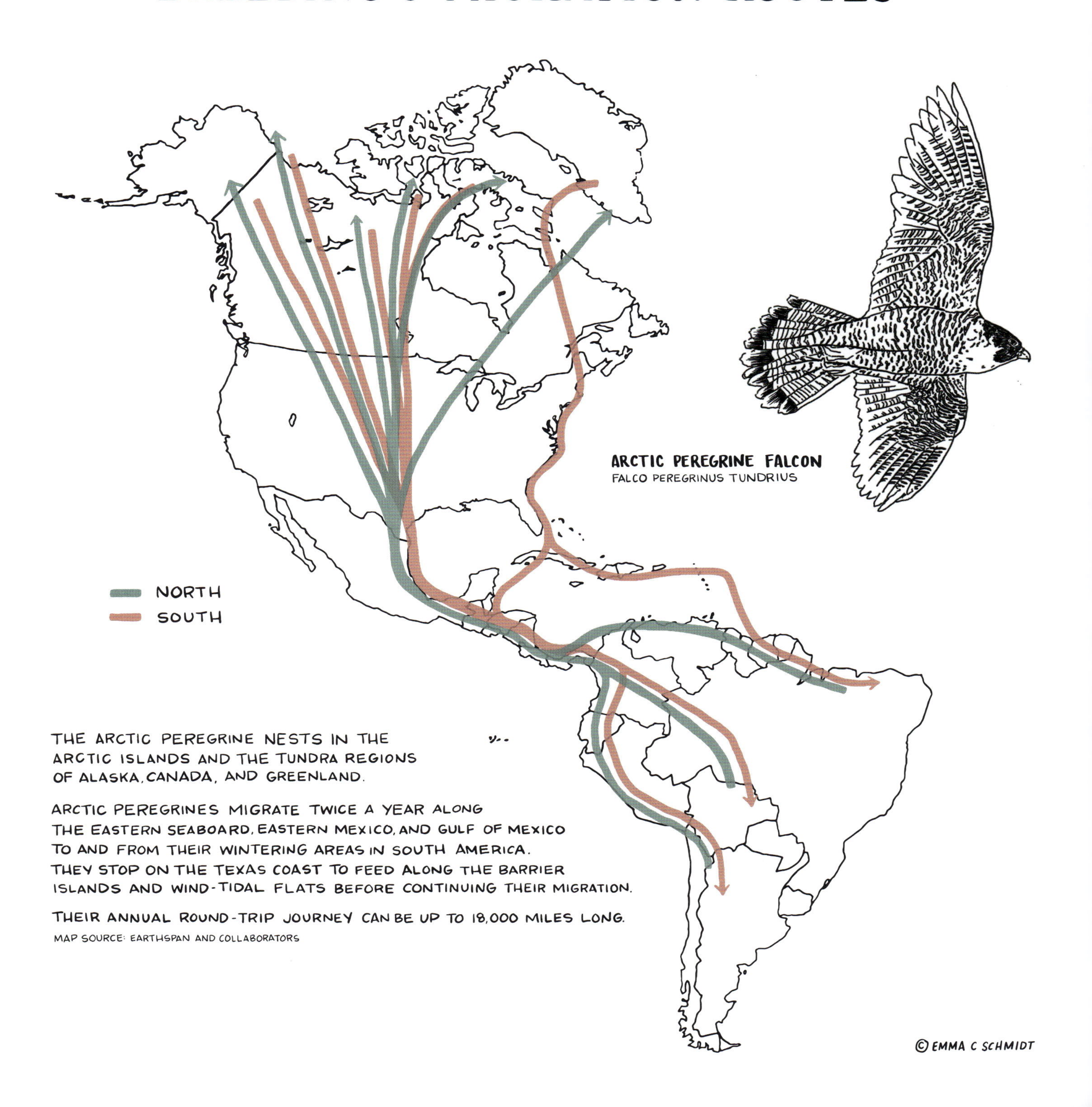

and human health concerns. During the surveys, they count, capture, band, collect tissue samples, and occasionally radio-mark and release the birds.

Sam and Gregg had captured one adult and one young female Peregrines who had hatched just months before. These birds are, as South Texas outdoor reporter Richard Moore coined, "three months old and 3,000 miles from home." Nineteen subspecies of Peregrine are recognized globally, three of which are native to North America—American, which is widespread in North America; Peale's of the northern Pacific coast and Islands; and Tundra or Arctic of the Alaskan, Canadian, and Greenlandic Arctic. During migration, Arctic Peregrines leapfrog over the range of continental nesting American Peregrine Falcons. Some will spend the winter on Padre Island, and others travel as far south as Chile or Argentina.

We visited late in the Peregrine migration period as the season was waning. The cold front that blew through a week ago, with strong southbound winds from the north, likely assisted the birds farther south along their migration routes. Arctic peregrines stop on Padre Island to rest and refuel during their migrations, along with many other Neotropical migrants. Peregrine migrants use Padre Island during both northbound and southbound migrations, which speaks to the importance and unique affinity of the Texas Gulf Coast to the species. The area provides food, water, resting, and ideal hunting habitats that Peregrines incorporate as stopovers into their long-distance migration strategies to complete their journeys.

These are some of the last Peregrines coming through on their way south. "Some will stop and winter here in South Texas," Gregg said, "and others will travel from the Arctic, stop over at Padre Island, and continue as far as Chile or Argentina. During spring migration, they'll revisit this circuit, upwards of a 16,000-mile round-trip journey."

RIGHT

(Top) Arctic Peregrine Falcon nestlings, during July at their eyrie ledge in West Greenland. Courtesy of Gregg Doney.

(Bottom) Chrissy and Gregg Doney of Earthspan prepare to release a juvenile Arctic Peregrine Falcon on South Padre Island.

Gregg and Sam also collected blood and feather samples for genetic analyses, monitoring contaminants like mercury levels and avian pathogens. They were talking about the fact that mercury cycles globally. It's in the air, and over decades, much of it ultimately settles in the permafrost in the Arctic. As the permafrost is melting rapidly due to global warming, mercury concentrates in the watershed runoff. The mercury cycles and biomagnifies through aquatic invertebrates to birds, and eventually, Peregrines may consume prey with high levels of mercury and get it into their bloodstream.

TRAIL RACING
SMITH

ABOVE
Sam Voss, a veteran Earthspan volunteer, collects tissue samples from an adult Arctic Peregrine Falcon on South Padre Island.

The Earthspan team and collaborators are tracking trends of mercury exposure in Peregrines to assess potential effects. According to Gregg, with a better understanding of the breeding/natal and winter origins of Peregrine migrants and their known associated molt patterns, researchers could relate mercury concentrations in specific feathers to breeding areas in the Arctic or wintering areas to isolate zones of exposure and then focus conservation efforts in those areas.

Earthspan's work has focused on understanding the natural history traits and behaviors to inform conservation and monitoring of the highly migratory Peregrine Falcon populations from the Arctic, where remnant but diminished Peregrine numbers held on through the decline of the 1950s and 1960s. As The Peregrine Fund's captive breeding and release program ramped up in the 1970s, Earthspan documented the decline of DDT residues in the blood of migrant Arctic Peregrines as improved breeding success steadily increased among Peregrine populations. These responses among Peregrines highlight the combined successes of active species management, associated research and monitoring, and DDT remediation efforts.

The Peregrine Fund and Earthspan's work to recover and restore Peregrine Falcons is a remarkable conservation success story. Because Peregrines are apex predators that prey on birds and focus their activity in important bird areas, they are also an ideal indicator species for assessing bird communities' health and habitat conditions. Earthspan and other groups' research and the long-standing background knowledge and data on an individual species, like Peregrine Falcons, can help inform current and future species and habitat conservation efforts in the Western Hemisphere. These concepts are particularly relevant in relation to the current associated conservation questions surrounding bird migration and distributions in changing environments. The Peregrine Fund is working hard to write an equally impressive comeback story for the Aplomado.

The Northern Aplomado Falcon was last seen in the American Southwest in the 1950s. The decline was linked to the conversion of open grasslands to farms, overgrazing, and brush encroachment that has swallowed their native habitat and nesting sites. Pesticides and nonselective poisoning of "nuisance" insects and animals also contaminated and decimated Aplomados' primary food sources, likely resulting in the loss of the remaining Aplomados in the United States. These factors ultimately landed the Aplomado Falcon on the U.S. Endangered Species List and the Texas Endangered Species List in 1986. It's the only falcon currently on the endangered species list in the United States.

The recovery of the Aplomado Falcon in the U.S. has involved a number of collaborations. In 1978, Grainger Hunt and colleagues at the Chihuahuan Desert Research Institute launched a successful captive breeding program with Aplomados they collected from Mexico. Eventually, that small captive flock was transferred to the Santa Cruz Predatory Research Group, which first released Aplomados to the wild in the 1980s as part of a pilot project. Using the same techniques to raise young and release them to their native habitat led to the successful recovery of the Peregrine Falcon.

Not long after the Aplomado Falcon was listed as endangered in 1986 and at the request of the U.S. Fish and Wildlife Service, The Peregrine Fund took on the task of recovering Aplomados in the United States on a much larger scale. Additional Aplomados were collected in Mexico in 1987 and 1988, and the captive population at Santa Cruz was transferred to The Peregrine Fund's breeding facility in Boise, Idaho, in 1990. Full-scale reintroductions of the falcon were initiated in 1993 in South Texas and later in the Desert Southwest of West Texas and New Mexico in 2002 and 2006.

South Texas' vast coastal prairies provide the perfect environment for Aplomados to thrive.

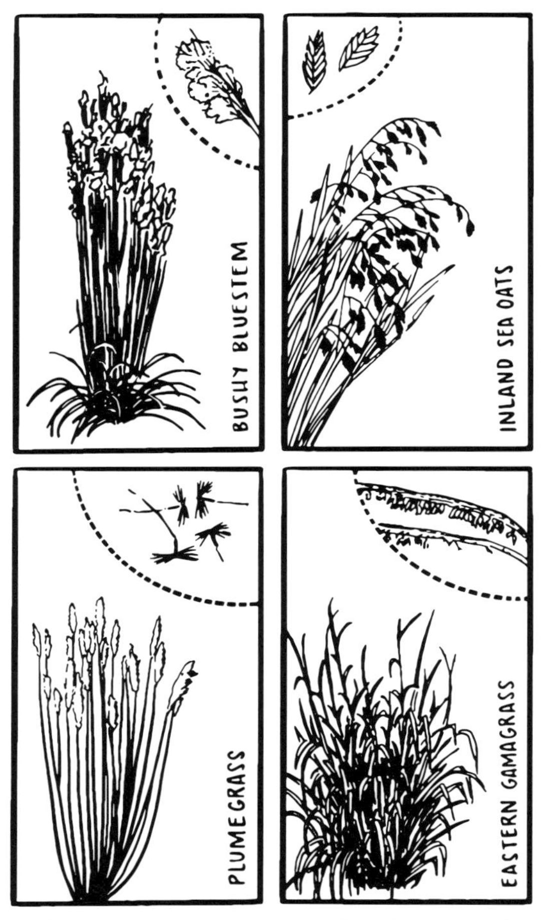

THE COASTAL PRAIRIE ONCE SPANNED 6.5 MILLION ACRES. TODAY, LESS THAN 1% OF TEXAS COASTAL PRAIRIE REMAINS. TEXAS' BARRIER ISLANDS AND PENINSULAS HOLD MUCH OF OUR REMAINING UNDISTURBED TRACTS OF COASTAL PRAIRIE. DEEP-ROOTED PRAIRIE GRASSES, LIKE THOSE ILLUSTRATED ABOVE, ALLOW WATER TO PERCOLATE INTO THE SOIL, HELPING TO STORE RAINFALL, PREVENT EROSION, AND SLOW OVERLAND WATER FLOW INTO STREAMS DURING STORMS.

THIS DIVERSE MOSAIC OF GRASSES AND FLOWERS PROVIDES IMPORTANT HABITAT FOR POLLINATORS, GRASSLAND BIRDS, AND MIGRATING WATERFOWL AND SHOREBIRDS.

The Texas coast was once home to six million acres of prairie, but by 1937, much of it had been lost to agriculture, residential development, and industry. The barrier islands and private ranches in South Texas hold most of the 1 percent of coastal prairie that survived. The open grasslands on Matagorda, San Jose, and Mustang Islands and ranch land between Corpus Christi and the Rio Grande River provide the perfect environment for Aplomados to thrive. Without trees and shrubs, mated pairs work together to flush out and pursue their prey—usually small birds and mammals, reptiles and large insects—at high speeds just above the grass line. Since Aplomados don't build their own nests, grasslands also provide the ideal conditions for other bird species, like hawks, to build nests big enough for Aplomado chicks.

The Peregrine Fund realized that protective nesting structures were essential to the raptors' success and that conserving large expanses of native habitat was equally as important. In 2013, the organization stopped captive breeding to focus on maintaining and expanding nesting sites and suitable habitats. The Peregrine Fund expanded the work it began in the 1980s by developing a network of private landowners and local, state, and federal agencies, with more than two million acres of land within the falcon's historic range.

Because Texas is more than 95 percent privately owned, access to private land is essential to the recovery of the species. Traditionally, landowners have had little legal or economic incentive to allow endangered species on their property and have had, in some respects, a disincentive to do so. The use of landowners' land by an endangered species brings with it the responsibility to avoid harming the species and its habitat. Responsibilities that can sometimes limit or modify land use alternatives.

RIGHT
Aplomado Falcon chicks in an artificial nest structure in South Texas.

To minimize their responsibilities under the Endangered Species Act, private landowners have historically refrained from taking actions that would benefit an endangered species. Some landowners may, in fact, take measures designed to reduce the likelihood that their land will be used by endangered fish or wildlife species in the future.

ABOVE
Chrissy, along with Paul Juergens and Brian Mutch with The Peregrine Fund, collect data.

The U.S. Fish and Wildlife Service created the Safe Harbor Agreement in 1995 to work with forest landowners in the Southeast to conserve endangered Red-cockaded Woodpeckers. The Agreement allows landowners to undertake activities that attract or otherwise benefit endangered species without fear that doing so will subject themselves and their land to new or additional regulatory restrictions.

Since then, hundreds of landowners have entered into such agreements covering millions of acres of forest, farm, and ranch land. Safe Harbor Agreements have been used to restore or enhance habitat and augment existing or new populations of dozens of endangered or threatened species in nearly every region of the country.

In 1996, at The Peregrine Fund's request, the U.S. Fish and Wildlife Service drafted a Safe Harbor Agreement for the Aplomado Falcon, which protected private landowners against any future restrictions placed on them or their land practices due to the presence of the endangered species on their property.

At the same time, it provided protection for the Aplomado Falcon, allowing biologists to choose the most suitable habitat for their research and restoration work. The assistance and support of private landowners who have signed on to Safe Harbor have helped make The Peregrine Fund's reintroduction efforts successful.

Just as drought impacted Aplomados in the Chihuahuan Desert, extreme weather set the Gulf Coast population back. In August 2017, Hurricane Harvey decimated the Aplomado population, then numbering 39 pairs, and destroyed many of The Peregrine Fund's artificial nests. During almost 30 years of The Peregrine Fund's recovery effort, some of the falcon population experienced hurricanes with little to no effect on the population. Harvey was different—it made landfall during the middle of the night, produced winds in excess of 120 mph, torrential rainfall, and a storm surge that crested barrier island dunes and submerged much of the falcon's low-lying habitat suitable for hunting. Hurricane Harvey erased one-third of the Texas coastal population of Aplomado Falcons.

ABOVE
Brian Mutch places a band on a chick.

After repairing and expanding the nest sites, continued work with land managers to improve and increase habitat, and re-engaging in small-scale, targeted reintroduction efforts, the organization sees signs of returning a resilient and growing population. Today, there are 23 breeding Aplomado Falcon pairs—one population on the barrier islands from Matagorda Island to Mustang Island and another around the Laguna Atascosa and Lower Rio Grande Valley National Wildlife Refuges near the Texas-Mexico border.

After decades of work, The Peregrine Fund's advanced computer analysis, the "Aplo-model," confirms that its approach is working: reproduction along the Texas Gulf Coast is ample to sustain a growing population in suitable habitat. Despite setbacks, the Aplomado Falcon is still on its way to becoming the last falcon removed from the endangered species list.

Chrissy and Brian Mutch holding young Aplomados before placing them back in their nesting structure.

Fund
KUIU

CHAPTER 9

CHASING THE TRASH

A TEXAS-SIZED PROBLEM

Day: 21
Miles walked: 370
Miles remaining: 0

October 21, 2023

We started at 7:30 a.m. on the north side of South Padre Island Beach, which is accessible by car. We were within view of condos, hotels, and most of the development on the island's southern tip.

Gene Gore joined us at the start to wish us luck on the final push and coordinate our boat ride from Padre to Boca Chica Beach.

We ran into a lot of people this morning. First was a couple in their truck. They drove in from Raymondville, saw us on the news the night before, and came out to say hello. Then we ran into someone working in Harlingen and staying in San Benito. He was a friend of a friend who'd been following us on social media, happened to be in the area, so he brought his dog,

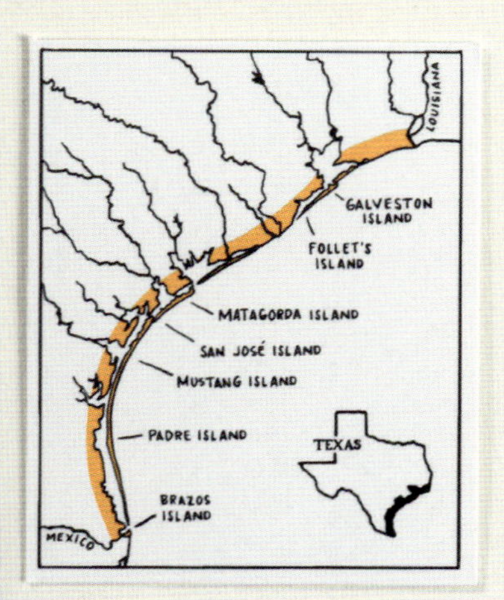

Jackalope, a.k.a. Jack along to see us. They walked with us for about a mile or so. We talked about the surprising clarity of the water and the sugar sand beach. We passed several beachside wedding setups with flower-adorned arches and rows of white chairs.

Jack and his owner doubled as our priest and witness for our pretend renewal of vows.

Once leaving the town of Padre Island just north of the National Seashore, we'd spent most of the past six days on beaches devoid of buildings and concentrations of people. Once we crossed underneath the long, elevated pier that marks the beginning of South Padre Island's pedestrian beach, we felt the sudden rush of civilization. High-rise condos and hotels lined the horizon. Families in bathing suits sat beside their coolers underneath sun shades, played paddleball, and swam.

And they stared at us. It didn't help that we were in running shoes, gators up to our shins, hiking pants, long-sleeved hooded fishing shirts, carrying sun umbrellas and backpacks, and keeping in rhythm with hiking poles. We looked like we were fresh off the Appalachian Trail.

We came across a family from nearby San Benito that, just five minutes before we walked by, were on Facebook and read about our journey. The dad yelled out, "Are you the Klebergs?" We went over and talked with them. The mother was celebrating her 70th birthday, and the son-in-law was celebrating his 50th. We took pictures with them, and Chrissy gave the mother a sundial shell. The father knew my dad. He told me that he had worked for the U.S.D.A. as a tick rider on the southern border in the 1970s and had done some side work for the King Ranch.

Gene gave us a ride to Brazos Island on a borrowed pontoon boat. We met Justin leClair on the other side. He's a biologist with Coastal Bend Bays and Estuaries Program. We walked and talked about

shorebirds and some of he and his colleagues work on the effects of SpaceX activity on local populations of Snowy, Wilson's, and Piping Plovers. The takeaway for both Chrissy and me was that the Boca Chica environment is essential as a stopover point for shorebirds

because of the algal mats and mud that hold many different organisms. The increased development and activity put pressure on the habitat and wildlife. They rely on this place for shelter, sustenance and shorebirds, in particular, depend on it as a stop on journeys thousands of miles long. We're putting all of that —

this wild place, the birds, migrations — in jeopardy.

We also realized that if we had finished a day late or a day early, we would not have been able to complete the journey within the three weeks we had alloted! SpaceX had closed public access to Boca Chica Beach on those days. It points to the importance of the Open Beaches Act and ensuring that we protect access. We've learned along the way that we wouldn't have been able to even do this walk without this act and public access to beaches in Texas. So, to end the trip at a time and place where access to a beach, the only beach in the region that doesn't require any paid parking sticker or entrance fee, is threatened was meaningful.

I got very emotional while Chrissy didn't want the journey to end. Once I finally stopped moving, the persistent stress

of trip planning, preparation, and execution hit me. I thought about how thankful I was to everyone who helped us along the way. In that moment, I ran through the memories of each day of the walk and realized that this was the end of a chapter.

But we're headed home to see the girls now and get back to being engaged in their daily lives. We have

a different perspective on our relationship, what's important in our lives, and the work we want to do. We both want this documentary series and all that comes of it to have a positive impact. We've met so many people who are excited about this project and love the coast. They just want others to feel the same.

One thing that David NEWSTEAD, Director of the Coastal Bird Program at Coastal Bend Bays and Estuaries Program once said to me is that we have to stop thinking about conserving these places and start thinking about enhancing them. What a total shift in mindset. We could see it at the beginning of our journey at McFaddin Beach, where partners are rebuilding the beaches and dunes. Hopefully, it's one of many things that comes out of this work — not just that people pay attention to the coast and think that it's beautiful, complex, culturally significant, and naturally rich, but that it's vital to our existence. We also have these string of barrier islands, these jewels, that are worth protecting and leaving better than we find them today.

A shoe washed ashore on the beach at Matagorda Peninsula.

A stranded Suburban on Matagorda Peninsula.

SUBURBA

Chrissy and I conducted trash surveys every 25 miles of our journey. At the start or end of each day, we picked a starting point on the beach and walked 100 meters at the new high tide line, logging debris within 5 meters on either side. In the first few days, it took us so long to write down our findings that we shifted to recording voice memos to make progress down the coast without pausing to write.

Our trash survey logs were provided by Jace Tunnel, director of community engagement at the Harte Research Institute for Gulf of Mexico Studies at Texas A&M University–Corpus Christi. The logs offer a glimpse of the variety of marine debris accumulating on our shores. Marine debris is any human-made solid material that ends up in oceans, seas, and other large bodies of water. There were 30 items on our trash log with three categories of plastic—hard, foamed, and film. We found every item listed on this list, although plastic in all forms dominated our surveys.

Jace established Nurdle Patrol in November 2018 after a plastic pellet spill on the Corpus Christi, Texas, beaches. By December 2023, over 9,000 citizen scientists from 25 countries had been surveying shorelines for tiny plastic pellets. The goal was to identify the source of the pellets and advocate for policy changes to prevent plastic pollution in the ocean.

We were interested in learning more about the larger pieces of plastic—bottles, bottle caps, shopping bags, and toys—we had been seeing so much throughout our journey. We arranged to meet up with Jace about midway on our walk while crossing Mustang Island. "There are two types of plastic we deal with on our coastline. Primary plastic is the raw material for all plastic items. We see these types of primary plastics on shorelines in the form of microbeads or nurdles, which look like miniature plastic BBs. Secondary plastics have already been made into a product. When those products get into the ocean, the sun degrades it and breaks it down over time," he explained. "Once it gets to be that small piece, usually anything under five millimeters, we call it microplastic.

"That plastic could be coming from anywhere—from a city in Texas, the middle of the U.S., from another country—travel down a river, out into the ocean, and then wash back up on the beach." He then described something I had seen on trash cleanup websites and anti-litter campaign flyers. Every piece of plastic that has ever been produced still exists in some shape or form. "Plastic doesn't dissolve. It just gets smaller and smaller over time.

RIGHT
A Ruddy Turnstone searches for food among the debris on Mustang Island.

ABOVE
Chrissy wearing an old motorcycle helmet she found on East Matagorda Peninsula.

Plastic waste has the most significant impact on wildlife, especially birds." As he said this, we watched a Sanderling scurry along the high tide line, digging for worms in the sand and eating colorful plastic fragments mixed in with the seaweed.

Tiny pieces of plastic can create abrasions in birds' digestive system, leading to infection and bleeding. If they consume enough, it can block their digestive system, make them feel full, and cause malnourishment. Although plastic may seem impervious, it can also absorb chemicals from the surrounding water, and those chemicals can then enter an animal's body if ingested. Fishing line and balloon strings can harm birds and other animals by entangling them. Shorebirds often get so tangled up in monofilament fishing line that they can't walk.

Marine debris endangers over 900 marine species, including sea turtles, algae, oysters, and fish. Sea turtles most commonly eat plastic sheeting and plastic bags, which resemble their jellyfish prey. Abandoned fishing gear can continue to catch fish and other marine life in a phenomenon known as ghost fishing. Algae can stick and grow on floating microplastics. Filter feeders such as oysters, scallops, and mussels consume both algae and microplastics simultaneously. These tiny plastic particles can then move up the food chain, being ingested by blue crabs and small fish, which are in turn eaten by larger predators like seals, sharks, and dolphins.

ABOVE
Jay wearing a pair of plastic glasses frames found on Matagorda Island.

Texas has 10 times the amount of trash on our beaches than anywhere else in the Gulf of Mexico.[1] Texas also has the highest average weight of trash debris per mile surveyed of any state in the nation.[2] Jace told us that this accumulation of litter is primarily due to the Loop Current. "It comes around the Yucatan Peninsula, goes up into the Gulf of Mexico, swings around the southern end of Florida, into the Gulf Stream, and then up the east coast of Florida. When that loop enters the eastern part of the Gulf of Mexico, it creates eddies that swirl off of it, which push against the Louisiana and Texas coastlines. The Loop Current is why we have the amount of debris that we have." Tunnel went on to say, as he stood in front of a Cuban refugee boat recently washed ashore, that trash gets swept into the Gulf of Mexico from Central and South America and from as far away as West Africa.

In addition to these currents and eddies, other factors contribute to the accumulation of debris on our shoreline. Year-round, winds approach the Texas coast from the east, currents run parallel to the coastline, and bring debris from Mexico and the Mississippi watershed, which drains all or part of 32 states, including parts of Texas and two Canadian provinces. Nearly every one of Texas' 30 million residents lives in a watershed that empties into the Gulf of Mexico. This means that in addition to trash from other parts of North America and the globe, the Gulf receives all of Texas' trash that ends up in a creek or river.

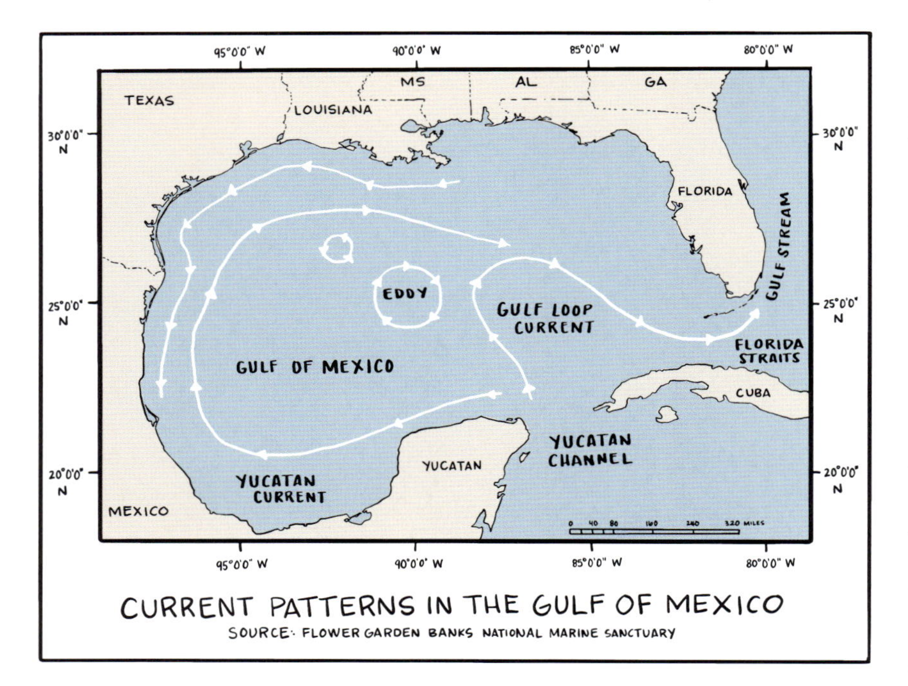

CURRENT PATTERNS IN THE GULF OF MEXICO

SOURCE: FLOWER GARDEN BANKS NATIONAL MARINE SANCTUARY

Chrissy easily logged an extra 20 miles on our 370-mile walk, as she zigzagged the tide line and upper beach every day in search of new trash. Sunglasses, baby strollers, swim goggles, hard hats, shipwrecked sailboats, and other interesting litter were just a fraction of the discarded items she found. Having lived through a lifetime of public awareness campaigns urging us to reduce, reuse, and recycle, cleaning up our coastline and oceans seemed insurmountable.

We asked Jace for some advice. "There are a few things we can all do. Get involved in a local community group that does trash cleanups. Think about your consumption—the things you're using daily. When you go to the grocery store, try to take a reusable bag, or do like I do and don't use any bags at all. Another thing we can all do is to drink from reusable water bottles. Ninety-nine percent of the water in the U.S. is safe and accessible from the tap or even out of your water hose. Don't use single-use plastic water bottles."

What are Texans doing to combat this accumulation of litter on our shores? In 2023, the Texas General Land Office's "Adopt-A-Beach" program recruited nearly 12,000 volunteers. Over the course of two coastwide cleanups that year, volunteers collected 154 tons and cleaned up 262 miles of Texas beach. Keep Texas Beautiful, a nonprofit, leads nearly 400 affiliates who reach 19 million Texans annually through litter prevention, waste reduction, and beautification. Thirty-two thousand volunteers cleaned up 288 miles of waterways and collected a total of 1 million pounds of trash and recyclable materials.

While Texans aren't solely responsible for the trash on our beaches, we play an oversized role in imagining a cleaner future.

MAJOR TEXAS RIVERS & RIVER BASINS

WYBOROWA

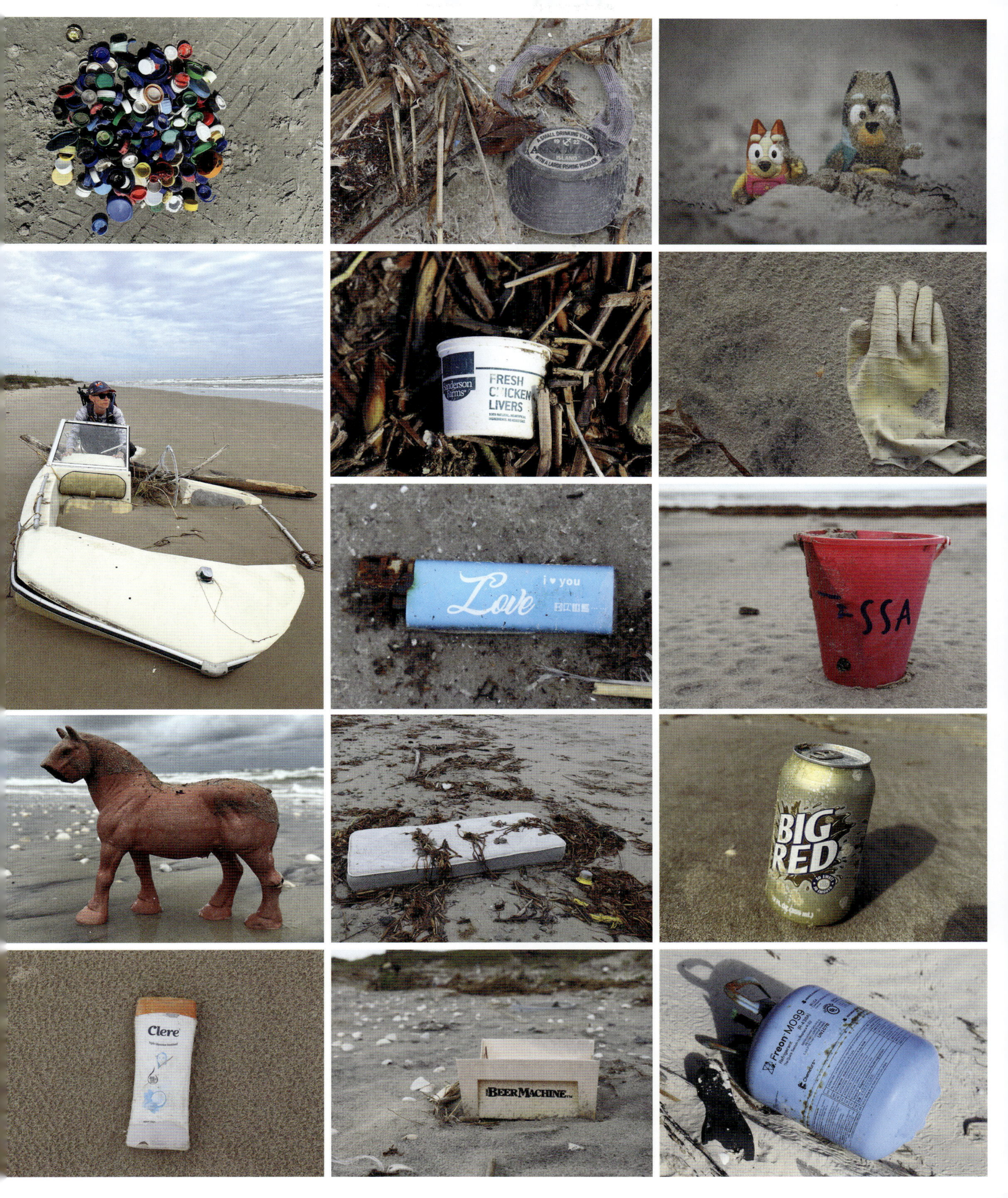
Sanderson Farms
FRESH CHICKEN LIVERS
Love
i ♥ you
SSA
BIG RED
Clere
BEER MACHINE
Freon MO99

vlasic
娃哈哈
桂圆莲子
BMC
LAW
1997-
2023

农夫山泉
NONGFU SPRING
Cleveland
LAUNCHER
400
8.5°
SUBMERGED
DANGER
PIPELINE
8
DK-9454-BA

CHAPTER 10

CONCLUSION

Jay walking in front of
a SpaceX rocket at
Boca Chica Beach.

A Sanderling runs back
and forth in sync with
the waves, searching for
prey in the wet sand.

Like the Ghost Wolves of Galveston Island, the Karankawa Kadla, or mixed Karankawa, have been hiding in plain sight, mainly surviving because of their mixed heritage. From 1250 AD to the mid-1800s, they controlled their narrow band of the Texas coast.

At their height, they likely numbered nearly 8,000 strong. They followed the rhythms of the seasons and lunar cycles, living in bands of up to 500 people in small villages along the coast in the spring and summer, subsisting on scallops, oysters, fish like red and black drum, trout, and sheepshead, as well as various plants like cattail, acorns, cactus, dewberries, and mesquite pods.[1]

During the fall and winter, they moved up to 60 miles inland to hunt bison and deer in smaller groups and traveled 200 miles to trade goods unique to the coast—seashells and naturally occurring tar. European colonizers depicted the Karankawas as the most savage First Peoples in Texas—a myth that unfortunately persists to this day.

Over time, their population dwindled due to appropriation, disease, displacement, and warfare. In the 1850s, after being forcibly removed from their homelands by Euro-American colonizers, the Karankawas integrated, out of a need for survival, into a changing society.

Surviving Karankawa peoples have retained and passed down aspects of their culture from generation to generation. Today, that history is becoming a living, breathing reality. Their descendants now have a tribal council and two clans—one centered in Corpus Christi and the other in Galveston.

In many ways, the Karankawa Kadla personify the Texas coast. For centuries, they migrated to and from the bays and barrier islands like the fluctuating tides. The Karankawa and the shallow bays thrived on the reliable exchange of fresh water from rivers and salt water from the Gulf. They are both underappreciated and misunderstood. The coast has been starved of fresh water since the 1950s, its wetlands reduced by half, and wild oyster reefs diminished due to overharvesting. To many Texans, the coast is an afterthought—home to oil and gas refineries, sleepy fishing villages, and crowded beach towns. Similarly, early

LEFT
Sovie, Cari, & Sunshine, members of the Karankawa Kadla from the Hawk Clan of Corpus Christi.

colonizers depicted the Karankawa as oversized cannibals and separated them from their life-giving homeland. They were more than overlooked, they were driven into the shadows.

Spanish explorer and mapmaker Captain Alonso Alvarez de Pineda and his crew were the first Europeans to map the Texas coastline, exploring present-day Corpus Christi Bay and the Rio Grande River in 1519. Nine years later, five boats with approximately 160 men on an expedition led by Pánfilo de Narváez landed separately between San Luis Pass and Mustang Island. Cabeza de Vaca was aboard one of the boats that ran ashore near Follet's Island, which they named "Isla de Malhado," or Island of Misfortune.

In September 1534, after four years on Follet's Island and a year as a captive of the Miriames and Iguaces, Cabeza de Vaca and three men escaped the barrier islands. They traveled for a year and a half through Texas and Northern Mexico until reaching the Spanish frontier outpost of Cuiliacan in April 1536. Although it would take another 150 years before Europeans revisited the Texas coast, the Spanish expeditions of the 1500s laid the foundation for a new era of colonization of the region.[2]

In February 1685, the French explorer René Robert Cavelier, Sieur de La Salle landed with 180 colonists at Matagorda Bay in Spanish-claimed territory. After the expedition's fourth and final ship, *La Belle*, sank with the remaining supplies in a storm, the colony they built inland from Lavaca Bay—today known as Fort St. Louis—only lasted until 1688. According to Stephen Hardin, a history professor at McMurry University in Abilene, "The Spaniards had no interest in the region north of the Rio Bravo until La Salle established his French colony there. Once they became aware of the settlement's existence, they made enormous efforts to eliminate it root and vine. Those efforts culminated in their missions, presidios, villas, vaqueros, and all the other trappings of Spanish culture. None of that would have occurred without La Salle."[3]

RIGHT
Coastal wetlands, like this one near High Island, cover much of Texas' undeveloped coastline.

In 1721 and 1722, the Spanish aimed to secure the region explored by La Salle by establishing a military fort, Presidio La Bahía, and a mission, Nuestra Señora de la Bahía del Espíritu Santo de Zúñiga, on Matagorda and Lavaca Bays. The last mission established in Texas was Nuestra Señora del Refugio in 1793. From March 12–15, 1836, the mission church, having been moved to the present-day site of Refugio, served as a fortress for Texans at the Battle of Refugio.

ABOVE
A family camping on the beach joined us as we made our way into Sargent.

As Texas gained its independence from Mexico and joined the union in the mid-19th century, Texans sought to connect every corner of the state. Immigrants and commercial goods arrived at the ports of Galveston, Indianola, Sabine Pass, and Velasco (present-day Surfside) and required connections inland. A chain of rivers and wetlands hindered the construction of permanent roads to link towns and ports along the coast's entire length. To navigate the coastline, travelers utilized ferries to cross barrier islands and the beaches as roads. The initial maps of the Texas highway system featured these beach roads.

Texas enshrined the right to unrestricted access to our coast, the front door to so much of our history. The 1959 Open Beaches Act, amended in 1991 and preserved in the Texas Constitution in 2009, states: "It is declared and affirmed to be the public policy of this state that the public, individually and collectively, shall have the free and unrestricted right of ingress and egress to and from the state-owned beaches."

The Texas coast, as in the time of the Karankawa, is still a gathering place. It is part of our state's origin story and is even more critical to our identity today. Texas is 95 percent privately owned, and most of the population now lives in cities. Our beaches are a great equalizer. They're free and accessible and provide rare opportunities to interact with each other and our shared history, regardless of background or belief.

Without the more than 600 beach access points and those who fight to keep that right, we would not have had the opportunity to meet so many people on our 21-day journey. We are indebted to those who helped us reach the Rio Grande and learn a little about the Texas Gulf Coast along the way.

A Ghost Crab on Matagorda Peninsula.

THE TEAM

Making a nonprofit documentary film series is like building a startup business with a limited lifespan and no chance of any financial return. In other words, it's a terrible business model but a hell of a lot of fun. What it lacks in profit, it makes up for in the chance to make a few friends and maybe make a difference. Like any new venture, *Chasing the Tide* began with an idea and a small group of passionate people.

In December 2023, Austin PBS leadership expressed interest in distributing a film about our walk of Texas' barrier islands. After meeting with their leadership team, they asked us to put a plan together and meet again in a month.

Our first call was to John Aldrich, with whom we'd worked on *The River and the Wall* and other smaller film projects. John has been making documentary films for 25 years. Originally from Florida, he attended the University of Texas at Austin's school of film and then earned a master's degree in documentary filmmaking from the University of Florida. He spent his early career in Washington, D.C., as a *National Geographic* producer/editor/shooter and then returned to Austin in 2010. John has edited three award-winning documentary features: *An Unreal Dream: The Michael Morton Story*, *Audubon*, and *The River and the Wall*. He has a talent for making complex stories cinematically gripping.

Chrissy and I met John for coffee and explained the project. John's initial questions centered on the logistics of the journey—crossing between islands, access to water and food, emergency evacuation plans, and covering the coast in just a few weeks. He had fewer concerns about filming and editing the project and made some suggestions about who could shoot it, put together the musical score, and handle the post-production aspects. We brainstormed the budget and discussed a fall 2024 premiere. After about an hour, we asked John if he'd join us as a co-producer, cinematographer, and editor on the project. Without hesitation, he accepted and agreed to join us for our follow-up meeting with Austin PBS.

RIGHT
John Aldrich spent time in the field and in the edit room bringing the story of the Texas coast to life.

ABOVE
Skip Hobbie on Chester Island. Skip's vision and cinematography experience were critical to the project's success.

Our next call was to Skip Hobbie. Chrissy, John, and I met Skip for lunch and described the project. Although Skip's expertise was shooting wildlife films, we knew he understood how to shoot in harsh conditions and could help us build a team of reliable cinematographers. He's filmed for *National Geographic*, BBC, Netflix, and PBS. He most recently served as director of photography on *Deep in the Heart: A Texas Wildlife Story* and as a producer and lead cinematographer on PBS Nature's film *Big Bend: The Wild Frontier of Texas*. Skip had spent some time on the Texas coast but was interested in doing more work there. We discussed the challenges—the elements would be hard on equipment, inclement weather could limit filming, and accessing Chrissy and me on 370 miles of remote barrier islands and peninsulas would be difficult. We offered Skip the director of cinematography role, which Chrissy and I didn't know was incorrect terminology. He accepted the offer, albeit with the correct title of director of photography.

A few weeks later, Chrissy met Karine Aigner at a RED camera workshop in California, and the two hit it off immediately. Karine mentioned that she was living on a ranch in South Texas, where she was photographing bobcats. Karine has been a freelance photographer since 2011, and her work has been featured in *National Geographic*, *Audubon* magazine, *Nature Conservancy Magazine*, and other publications. In 2022, Karine became the fifth woman in 58 years to win the grand prize title in the Natural History Museum of London's Wildlife Photographer of the Year competition, which showcases the world's best nature photography and photojournalism. Chrissy invited Karine on our first shoot to film redhead ducks on the Laguna Madre, and she then joined the team during pre-production in Galveston and High Island. Although she was busy traveling across the Western Hemisphere, she joined us for the first few days of our journey in October 2023 from Texas Point National Wildlife Refuge to Galveston Island. Her photos were an invaluable contribution to this project.

ABOVE
Karine Aigner is a world-class photographer. She captured key parts of the journey and some of the coast's iconic wildlife species.

ABOVE
Henry Davis (left) and Patrick Thrash (right) ventured to the most remote barrier islands to get breathtaking shots and document the hardships of the journey.

Henry Davis joined the project at Skip Hobbie's recommendation. In the spring of 2023, Henry spent a week filming Ghost Wolves on Galveston Island and captured every shot of the elusive canids we used for the film series and this book. He spent another week that summer filming Kemp's ridleys in South Padre Island and 15 of 21 days filming during the walk of the Texas coast in October. Henry has a knack for getting difficult shots and bringing out the best in his subjects.

I worked with Patrick Thrash on *Deep in the Heart: A Texas Wildlife Story*. He is a native of the Texas Hill Country and has lived and worked as far away as Hungary and Mexico. His passion for people, wildlife, and wild places led him to pursue work as a guide, photographer, and cinematographer after attending Texas A&M University. Patrick quickly learned how to handle a camera in the field and has compiled a resume that includes *National Geographic*, BBC, and PBS projects. He filmed at High Island during pre-production, and in October, he captured footage during stormy weather on the Upper Coast and the remote beaches of East Matagorda and Matagorda Peninsula.

ABOVE

Stephanie DeWaters (left) developed communications for the film series and recruited new audiences to learn about the coast. Katherine Hill (right) managed production and was instrumental in keeping the team on schedule and on task.

Stephanie DeWaters came to the team at the recommendation of our friends at Harte Research Institute. Stephanie is a native Texan and a Padre Island resident, and she has spent most of her life along the South Texas coast. She holds a marketing degree from Texas A&M University–Corpus Christi and is deeply passionate about promoting coastal conservation initiatives and wildlife rehabilitation. We consistently counted on Stephanie when we got into binds during the walk of the southern part of the coast—helping to coordinate a beachfront dinner for 30 people on Mustang Island, finding a kayak for us to cross Packery Channel, and coordinating our first television interview at Padre Island National Seashore.

Without Katherine Hill, we could not have completed the 21-day journey and coordinated interviews, lodging, meals, and transportation. Kat signed on as *Chasing the Tide*'s production manager in August 2023 and was the perfect fit for the job. She was raised in Corpus Christi, has a degree in geography, and has experience in commercial film production. Kat kept the production rolling down the coast and on schedule through the heat, rain, unplanned river crossings, and long days.

ABOVE
(Left) Landry Gideon ensured that we had the best audio in the most challenging conditions. (Right) Making movies and books is a team effort.

RIGHT
Ellis Pickett, founder of the Texas chapter of the Surfrider Foundation, was an invaluable addition to the team.

One thing any documentary film series worth its salt cannot do without is quality sound. Enter Landry Gideon, sound mixer and boom operator. Landry joined us in South Padre and Port Aransas, where the wind, elements, and boat-based interviews made for challenging conditions. Landry is a graduate of the University of Texas at Austin film school and produced and directed the feature-length documentary *One Act Play,* a film about high school drama. He most recently worked on shows for HBO, MAX, and A&E.

Thank you to everyone who helped us reach Boca Chica and breathed life into this project. We love the Texas Gulf Coast and the people who give it its character.

WARNING
4-WHEEL DRIVE
HIGH-CLEARANCE VEHICLES ONLY.
TOWING SERVICES ARE VERY EXPENSIVE!
Driving conditions change on a regular basis.
" Be aware of tides, soft sand and debris."
SKY ISLAND

Thank you to our generous donors and
volunteers for believing in this project
and making it a reality.

DONORS

- Caesar Kleberg Foundation for Wildlife Conservation
- J.W. Couch Foundation
- Caesar Kleberg Wildlife Research Institute
- Texas Parks & Wildlife Foundation
- Harte Research Institute for Gulf of Mexico Studies at Texas A&M-Corpus Christi
- Gulf of Mexico Trust
- Threshold Foundation
- Shield-Ayres Foundation
- Alice Kleberg Reynolds Foundation
- Gossamer Gear
- Texas Water Foundation
- Rambler Sparkling Water
- Jenny Ahearn
- Helen Alexander
- Scott Atlas
- Matthew Baker
- Sally Bowden
- Patrick Buckley
- Dick Butler
- Charles C. Butt
- Anne & Cameron Campbell
- Leonidas Cartwright
- Blair & Wade G. Chappell
- Scott Chase
- George Cofer
- Terry Cook
- Fannie Davis
- Carol Dawson
- June Deadrick
- Michael Deane
- Dalton DeHart
- Claire Dewar
- Cheryl & Paul Drown
- Gilda Wise Duffy
- Cary Dupuy
- Tom Fitzpatrick
- Cina Alexander Forgason
- Pam and Will Harte
- James H. Hazen
- Jeffrey Hill
- John Hinton
- Emily House
- Robert Howard
- Julia Jitkoff
- Kay and RossIrby
- Kathryn Kitchen
- Sally S. Kleberg
- Kevin Kosch
- Veda Kull
- John Langmore
- Nan Lefforge
- Byron Lemmond
- Ken Luce
- Kim Ludeke
- Ben Masters
- Taddy McAllister
- Deborah McBride
- Margo McClinton
- Dan McCullar
- Mona Mehdy
- Myfe Moore
- Tracy LaQuey Parker
- Julie Summerford Pearson
- Mark Phariss
- Shirley Rich
- Louise Rosenfield
- Chula Ross Sanchez
- Mary E. Schultz
- Stuart Schwartz
- Susan Seeds
- George Shackelford
- Susan Smith
- Dede Spontak
- Jackie Stewart
- David Todd
- Suzanne M. Tuttle
- Russell Waddill
- Carol Watts
- Lin Weber
- Kathleen Wilson
- Emily Wong

THANK YOU

- Austin Alvarado
- Bart Ballard, PhD
- Paula Baker
- Alexis Baldera
- Chelsey Ballarte
- Sunshine Beaumont
- Michel Bechtel
- John Blaha
- Jim Blackburn
- Amy Bonka, PhD
- Michelle Booth
- Jeb Boyt
- Mark Boyt
- Judge Jeff Branick
- Anne Brown
- Eric Brunnemann
- Kristin Brzeski, PhD
- Ellen Burris
- Juan Canchola
- Tony Carroll
- Chris Carson
- Heather Cooley
- Tim Cooper
- Ernie Crenwelge
- Josh Davis
- Carlo Defrancis
- Pete Deichmann
- Jimmy Deloache
- Stephanie DeWaters
- Gregg Doney
- Gene Fisseler
- Michael Fojtasek
- Joe Fox
- Rodney Franklin
- Lawrence Getwood Jr.
- Richard Gibbons
- Adam Gonzales
- Gene Gore
- Ava Graves
- Terry Hadley
- Greg Hall
- Cullen Hanks
- Terry Harris
- Douglas Head
- Rob Hein
- Josh Henderson
- Jeremiah Herrera
- Dave Hewitt, PhD
- Audrey Hill
- Paul Hobby
- Anna Margaret Hollyman
- Michael Isbell
- Ed James
- Chantal James
- Freddy Johnston
- Parker Johnson
- Brud Jones
- Paul Juergens
- Randall Kempner
- Shrub Kempner
- Cristina Kenny
- Steve Kimbley
- Karla Klay
- Tio Kleberg
- Chris Kleberg
- Janell Kleberg
- Wendy Knight
- Weston Koehler
- Vanessa Kramer
- Evangelina Kreeger
- Chris Kuchinski
- Phil Lamb
- John Langmore
- Holly Lazenby
- Kjell Lindgren, PhD

- Ernesto Lopez
- Jose Lopez
- Elizabeth Lorenz
- Laurie Lyng
- Jamal Marshall
- Jimmy McBee
- Emily McCauley
- Chris McFaddin
- Larry McKinney, PhD
- James Musick
- Michelle Musick
- Brian Mutch
- Chuck Naiser
- Lisa Neely
- David Newstead
- Missy Nichols
- Kyle O'Haver
- Cari Ortega
- Sovie Ortega
- Carmen Osier
- Terry Palmer, PhD
- Chris Parish
- Ben Paschal
- Luis Patiño
- Alex Perez
- Ellis Pickett
- Jennifer Pollack, PhD
- Felipe Prieto
- Timothy Pylate
- Megan Radke
- Pickle Ragusin
- Justin Rhodes
- Shirley Rich
- Dennis Rich
- Robin Riechers
- Bruce Roberts
- Sara Robertson
- Natalie Rosado
- Wade Ruddock
- April Russell
- Allison Ryan
- Sandra Sanchez
- Andrew Sansom, PhD
- Bailey Schacht
- Tim Seiter
- Julie Shaddox
- Megan Stewart
- Bob Stokes
- Greg Stunz, PhD
- Gail Sutton
- Romey Swanson
- Scott Taylor
- Jace Tunnell
- Homer Villareal
- Joshua Villareal
- Christian von Preysing
- Bridgett vonHoldt, PhD
- Sam Voss
- Dan Walker
- Frank Ward
- Jim Ward
- Peggy Wilkinson
- Tim Wilkinson
- Sarah Wilson
- Jesse Womack
- Ron Wooten
- Absolem Yetzirah
- Mariposa Yetzirah
- David Yoskowitz, PhD
- Stella Yrigoyen
- Sanjuana Zavala

ENDNOTES

CHAPTER 1: THE CHENIER PLAIN

1. Caudle, Tiffany, Paine, Jeffrey G., and Mathew, Sojan (2011, July). *Texas Gulf Shoreline Change Rates Through 2007.* Bureau of Economic Geology - John A. and Katherine G. Jackson School of Geosciences at The University of Texas at Austin. https://www.beg.utexas.edu/files/publications/contract-reports/CR2011-Paine-2.pdf.

CHAPTER 2: HIGH ISLAND

1. Cornell University (2019, January 9). Two billion birds migrate over Gulf Coast. ScienceDaily. www.sciencedaily.com/releases/2019/01/190109110058.htm.
2. Kellman, Ryan and Hersher, Rebecca (2023, April 10). Why Texans need to know how fast Antarctica is melting. NPR. https://apps.npr.org/arctic-ice-melting-climate-change/texas-galveston-sea-level-rise.html#:~:text=Hanzhang%20Jin%2FNPR-,There%20has%20been%20more%20than%202%20feet%20of%20sea%20level,inches%20of%20sea%20level%20rise.&text=All%20that%20water%20is%20threatening,being%20destroyed%20by%20rising%20seas.
3. The Meadows Center for Water and the Environment (2024, January 18). Sea Level Rise. https://www.meadowscenter.txst.edu/climatechange/climatedashboard/sealevelrise.html.
4. Yoskowitz, PhD David W., Gibeaut, PhD James, and McKenzie, Ali (June 2009). *The Socio-Economic Impact of Sea Level Rise in the Galveston Bay Region: A report for Environmental Defense Fund.* Harte Research Institute for Gulf of Mexico Studies Texas A&M University–Corpus Christi. https://www.edf.org/sites/default/files/9901_EDF_Sea_Level_Rise_Report.pdf.
5. Rosenberg, Kenneth V. et al. (2019, September 19) Decline of the North American avifauna. *Science* vol. 366, no. 1641, 120–124. https://www.science.org/doi/10.1126/science.aaw1313.

CHAPTER 3: GHOST WOLVES

1. Morell, Virginia (2016, July 27). How do you save a wolf that's not really a wolf? *Science*. https://www.science.org/content/article/how-do-you-save-wolf-s-not-really-wolf.
2. vonHoldt, Bridgett M. et al. (2016, July 27) Whole-genome sequence analysis shows that two endemic species of North American wolf are admixtures of the coyote and gray wolf. *Science Advances*, vol. 2, no. 7. https://www.science.org/doi/10.1126/sciadv.1501714.
3. Graves, Russell A. (2019, December). Mystery Canines of Galveston Island. *Texas Parks and Wildlife Magazine*. https://tpwmagazine.com/archive/2019/dec/ed_3_wolves/index.phtml.
4. Heppenheimer E., Brzeski K.E., Wooten R., Waddell W., Rutledge L.Y., Chamberlain M.J., Stahler D.R., Hinton J.W., and vonHoldt B.M. (2018, December 10). Rediscovery of Red Wolf Ghost Alleles in a Canid Population Along the American Gulf Coast. *Genes* vol. 9, no.12: 618. https://doi.org/10.3390/genes9120618.
5. Samuels, Fionna M. D. (2022, October 5). Rediscovered Red Wolf Genes May Help Conserve the Species. *60-Second Science* podcast [Audio podcast]. *Scientific American*. https://www.scientificamerican.com/podcast/episode/rediscovered-red-wolf-genes-may-help-conserve-the-species/.

CHAPTER 4: BARRIER ISLANDS

1. Randall, Keith (2020, October 27). Texas A&M Expert: Storms Worsening State's Beach Erosion. Texas A&M Today. Problem. https://today.tamu.edu/2020/10/27/texas-am-expert-storms-worsening-states-beach-erosion-problem.

CHAPTER 5: OYSTERS

1. Pollack, PhD Jennifer Beseres, and Sutton, M.S. Gail (2019, July 9). Shell Bank: Oyster shell recycling, community involvement, student institute, and oyster health, Final Report for GLO Contract # 18-093-000-A604, 46. https://www.glo.texas.gov/coastal-grants/_documents/grant-project/18-093-final-rpt.pdf.
2. Hynes, Thomas (2022, August 4). Aw Shucks: The Tragic History of New York City Oysters. Untapped New York. https://untappedcities.com/2022/08/04/history-new-york-oysters.
3. Pelton, Tom, Goldsborough, Bill (2010, July). On the Brink: Chesapeake's Native Oysters - What it Will Take to Bring Them Back. Chesapeake Bay Foundation. https://www.cbf.org/document-library/cbf-reports/Oyster_Report_for_Release02a3.pdf.
4. Pollack, PhD Jennifer Beseres, and Sutton, M.S. Gail (2019, July 9). Shell Bank: Oyster shell recycling, community involvement, student institute, and oyster health, Final Report for GLO Contract # 18-093-000-A604, 50. https://www.glo.texas.gov/coastal-grants/_documents/grant-project/18-093-final-rpt.pdf.
5. Barer, David (2013, May 28). A Brief History of the Texas Water Plan. NPR. https://stateimpact.npr.org/texas/2013/05/28/a-brief-history-of-the-texas-water-plan.
6. Henson, Margaret Swett (1993, January). The History of Galveston Bay Resource Utilization. The Galveston Bay National Estuary Program. Publication GBNEP-39, 57. https://tamug-ir.tdl.org/bitstreams/7d602cf2-f186-48cf-b616-65d7c82ffd74/download.
7. Shrake, Edwin (1967, August 14). Dredging up a Texas Squabble: A Few People Have Been Making A Lot of Money By Taking Oyster Shells From Galveston Bay. Conservationists Maintain That The Practice is Decimating the Live Beds and Polluting the Waters. *Sports Illustrated*. https://vault.si.com/vault/1967/08/14/dredging-up-a-texas-squabble.
8. National Audubon Society, Inc. v. Johnson, 317 F. supp. 1330 (S.D. Tex. 1970). Justia Law. (n.d.). https://law.justia.com/cases/federal/district-courts/FSupp/317/1330/1415359/.
9. Hicks, Tacey, PhD Candidate in Oceanography at Texas A&M University, and Shamberger, Kathryn, Associate Professor of Oceanography at Texas A&M University (2023, November 14). Hurricane Harvey More than Doubled the Acidity of Texas' Galveston Bay, Threatening Oyster Reefs. The Conversation. https://theconversation.com/hurricane-harvey-more-than-doubled-the-acidity-of-texas-galveston-bay-threatening-oyster-reefs-196470.

CHAPTER 6: REDHEADS AND THE LAGUNA MADRE

1. Sands, J.P., DeMaso, S.J., Schnupp, M.J., and Brennan, L.A. (Eds.). (2012). *Wildlife Science: Connecting Research with Management* (1st edition). CRC Press, 112, https://doi.org/10.1201/b12139.
2. Last Will and Testament of Caesar Kleberg as cited in Leach, Duane M. (2017). *Caesar Kleberg and the King Ranch* (1st edition). Texas A&M University Press, 278.

CHAPTER 7: KEMP'S RIDLEY

1. Adams, D.E. (1966). More About the Ridley, Operation: Padre Island Egg Transplanting. *International Turtle and Tortoise Society Journal* vol. 1: 18–45.
2. National Park Service (2023). The Story of the Kemp's Ridley. Padre Island National Seashore. https://www.nps.gov/pais/learn/nature/kempsridleystory.htm#:~:text=In%201951%2C%20the%20first%20published,of%20Mexico%20at%20that%20time.

CHAPTER 8: NORTHERN APLOMADO FALCONS

1. Hunt, W. Grainger, Jessi L. Brown, Tom J. Cade, John Coffman, Marta Curti, Erin Gott, William Heinrich, et al. (2013, December 1). Restoring Aplomado Falcons to the United States." *Journal of Raptor Research* vol. 47, no. 4, 335–351. https://doi.org/10.3356/JRR-12-52.1.

CHAPTER 9: CHASING THE TRASH

1. Caitlin Wessel, Kathleen Swanson, and Tracy Weatherall, Just Cebrian (2018, December 18). Accumulation and distribution of marine debris on barrier islands across the northern Gulf of Mexico. *Marine Pollution Bulletin*, vol. 139, 14–22. https://doi.org/10.1016/j.marpolbul.2018.12.023.
2. Hardesty, Britta Denise, Chris Wilcox, Qamar Schuyler, TJ Lawson and Kimberley Opie. (2017) Developing a baseline estimate of amounts, types, sources and distribution of coastal litter – an analysis of US marine debris data. Version 1.2.

CHAPTER 10: CONCLUSION

1. Ricklis, Robert A. (1996) *The Karankawa Indians of Texas: an ecological study of cultural tradition and change*. University of Texas Press, 101–110.
2. Carson, David (2021, December 1). The Narvaez Expedition. TexasCounties.net. https://www.texascounties.net/articles/discovery-of-texas/narvaezexpedition.htm.
3. Theis, David (2021, May 21). The Tragic Tale of a 17th-Century French Colony's Collapse. Texas Highways. https://texashighways.com/culture/history/the-tragic-tale-of-a-17th-century-french-colonys-collapse/.

ABOUT THE AUTHORS

JAY KLEBERG

Jay is the executive director of the Gulf of Mexico Trust and previously served as associate director of Texas Parks Wildlife Foundation. He co-produced the documentary film *Deep in the Heart: A Texas Wildlife Story* and was associate producer of *The River and the Wall.*

CHRISSY KLEBERG

Chrissy is a former wildlife field biologist and photographer. She has conducted avian research and reintroduction work with the U.S. Geological Survey, University of Florida, and The Peregrine Fund in Hawaii, Florida, New Mexico, and Texas.

Chrissy and Jay co-directed and co-produced the *Chasing the Tide* documentary series. They live in Austin with their three daughters.